Catherine Marshall

WOMEN OF FAITH SERIES

Amy Carmichael
Catherine Marshall
Corrie ten Boom
Fanny Crosby
Florence Nightingale
Gladys Aylward

Isobel Kuhn
Joni
Madame Guyon
Mary Slessor
Susanna Wesley

MEN OF FAITH SERIES

Andrew Murray
Borden of Yale
Brother Andrew
C. S. Lewis
Charles Colson
Charles Finney
Charles Spurgeon
D. L. Moody
E. M. Bounds
Eric Liddell
George Muller
Hudson Taylor
Jim Elliot

John Calvin
John Hyde
John Newton
John Paton
John Wesley
Jonathan Goforth
Luis Palau
Martin Luther
Oswald Chambers
Samuel Morris
William Booth
William Carey

WOMEN AND MEN OF FAITH

John and Betty Stam
Francis and Edith Schaeffer

OTHER BIOGRAPHIES FROM BETHANY HOUSE

Autobiography of Charles Finney
George MacDonald: Scotland's Beloved Storyteller
Hannah Whitall Smith
Help Me Remember, Help Me Forget (Robert Sadler)
Janette Oke: A Heart for the Prairie
Miracle in the Mirror (Nita Edwards)
Of Whom the World Was Not Worthy (Jakob Kovac family)

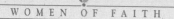

WOMEN OF FAITH

Catherine Marshall

Kathy McReynolds

BETHANY HOUSE PUBLISHERS
MINNEAPOLIS, MINNESOTA 55438

Catherine Marshall
Copyright © 1999
Kathy McReynolds

Published by Bethany House Publishers
A Ministry of Bethany Fellowship International
11400 Hampshire Avenue South, Minneapolis, Minnesota 55438
www.bethanyhouse.com

Printed in the United States of America by
Bethany Press International, Minneapolis, Minnesota 55438

ISBN 0–7642–2167–1

This book is lovingly dedicated to
my beloved husband,
Mike,
and my three beautiful children,
Jessica Kathcrinc
Moriah Nicole
Jeremiah Michael

"My cup runneth over."

KATHY McREYNOLDS is a graduate of Biola University and Talbot School of Theology (M.A.). She has coauthored several books and contributed to several collections. She lives in California with her husband and children.

Contents

Introduction

Catherine Marshall was one of the deepest, most provocative Christian women of the twentieth century. A spiritual giant she was—but one who was also painfully aware of her weaknesses and shortcomings. Through the years, those who read Catherine's works grew to love her, this woman who intimately and honestly bared her soul. They laughed with her. They cried with her. Most importantly, they learned to trust the Lord with her.

In the pages of this book, you'll meet Catherine Marshall, a complicated and fascinating woman. You'll meet her as a little girl who dared to dream God's dreams. You'll meet her as a teenager who dared to ask tough questions, not fearing the answers. You'll meet her as a young woman whose husband was the apple of her eye. When that apple fell to the ground, she also crashed.

You'll meet her as a woman who, from the dust and ashes of her life, lifted her eyes toward heaven and was raised to her feet. When she was raised up, she walked steadily toward His light. Though at times the circumstances of life shrouded her journey with bleak darkness, she steadfastly stood her ground, determined to stay on His path.

You'll meet her as a woman who said "yes" to a second chance at happiness. Through this experience, God brought her to new heights of spiritual maturity. But there were many hills and valleys along the way. Before it was over, she learned to love and to accept love as she never had before.

You'll meet her as a mature woman who challenged the status quo as far as faith was concerned, only to have circumstances backfire in her face. The pain of this experience was excruciating. But through it all she anchored herself firmly in the Lord of love. Ultimately, this tragedy brought her to the foot of the Cross, where she made the "great exchange" with her Lord.

Catherine Marshall was truly a unique woman. Her life and writings testify to this fact. As much as an imperfect human being could, Catherine Marshall lived Christ. Many of her personal journal entries and writings, which are integrated into this book, invite you to "taste and see that the Lord is good." By using these select passages from her literary works, this book captures the essence of Catherine Marshall's spiritual journey. Our hope is that you come to a deeper knowledge of the Lord of Life through this remarkable woman's testimony.

1

The Early Years

How can I love someone I'm afraid of?" asked young Catherine as she gazed into the loving eyes of her father, John Wood. "Because He loves you," he answered. "We love Him because He first loved us. He loved you before you even knew He was there."[1] Catherine, who adored her father, usually took his counsel and tucked it away in her heart. But this time his teaching was beyond her understanding.

"But I can't feel it [God's love], or hear any words, or see a face full of love like I see your face, Dad,"[2] responded Catherine. Because of this, God felt distant and unreal to her. She could not understand how He, who is unseen and unheard, could love her. To her young mind, love—for it to be love—had to be tangible. It had to have a voice. It had to have hands and feet.

To put it simply, for Catherine, love had to be a touchable reality. This is because she learned to know

---

[1] Catherine Marshall, *Meeting God at Every Turn: A Spiritual Autobiography*, reprint. ed. (Grand Rapids, Mich.: Chosen Books, 1995), 21.
[2] Ibid.

it, to hear it, and to feel it through her parents' patient and compassionate actions. Throughout her childhood years, she wrapped herself in their love and was secure in their presence.

But this consistent, loving input from her parents did not keep Catherine from every emotional challenge. She often went through periods when she was shy, withdrawn, and plagued by feelings of inferiority.

Sarah Catherine was born in 1914 and lived in at least four different places as a child: Greenville, Tennessee; Umatilla, Florida; Canton, Mississippi; and Keyser, West Virginia. She was an only child until the age of seven, when she welcomed into her world her brother, Bob, and fourteen months later, her sister, Emmy. Her father, John Ambrose Wood, was a Presbyterian minister. He was a tall and handsome man, full of good humor, and gentle in spirit. Her mother, Leonora Whitaker Wood, stayed at home, ministering to her family, the congregation, and the community. She also was tall and very lovely, graced with alluring blue eyes and a captivating smile.

Because he chose to have his office at home, Catherine was able to spend as much time with her father as she needed. It was during these early years that she developed a close, intimate relationship with him. His office door and his arms were always open to her. Even if he had someone in his office, Catherine was welcome to sit quietly on his lap.

John Wood was an openly warm and sociable man, whose great love was his ministry to people. On one occasion, while living in Keyser, West Virginia, he went to the railroad yards to visit a new member of his congregation. The gentleman told his new pastor that he could not shake hands at the moment because they were too dirty.

John bent down and soiled his hands in the mud and said, "Can you shake hands with me now?" He treated his entire flock with the same kind of dignity and respect, which is why he was so well-liked by all who came in contact with him. He was accessible and could always find some common interest with the ordinary person.

But his love for his congregation never caused him to neglect the needs of his family. He was never too busy to play games or to help with schoolwork or to simply give a hug when it was needed. Of course, Reverend Wood had his share of weaknesses. For example, he could be quite stubborn at times.

He also loved to tinker with tools, and he would often spend more money than he should on little gadgets to work on mechanical projects or on the yard. He once saw a flamethrower being advertised and thought it was just the thing he needed. When his wife protested, he firmly told her that he was going to buy it anyway.

Mr. Wood also displayed on occasion a volatile temper. One winter he was stringing up some Christmas lights on the roof and accidentally slipped, hitting his hand with a hammer. He let some very irreverent words slip from his tongue in front of his young son, Bob. He quickly instructed his son to forget he heard such words. Of course, Bob did not forget. Instead, he immediately told his sister what had happened.

Catherine's response was surprising. She loved and respected her father all the more because he was not "too good to be human." She often reflected on these times with her father as the happiest season in her young life.

However, at the same time there was tension in her soul because the God whom her father worshiped was a mystery to her. She put it this way: "And so at an early age I knew I could trust my earthly father. But I resisted the sermons that urged us to surrender our lives to a faraway God. What did that mean? The idea of spending all my time praying, reading the Bible, and talking about God did not appeal to me at all."[3]

Not long after this, however, an evangelist named Gypsy Smith came to town to hold revival meetings. On a particular Sunday, Catherine attended one of these meetings and was deeply moved by the power of his preaching. She was at the same time puzzled by the experience and unsure about what it meant to "give your life to God."

Later that Sunday, while listening to her father preach, Catherine sensed the call of God. And, much to her surprise, she responded. The following is her recollection of this event:

> At the end of the service, rather spontaneously as I recall, Dad issued an invitation for those to come forward who wanted to accept Jesus as the Lord of their life and to be a part of the church fellowship.
>
> And suddenly I felt a stirring inside me. Very gentle. There was no voice or words, just a feeling of great warmth. I loved my father dearly. And I trusted him with all my heart. I loved him so much that I could feel tears forming behind my eyes. And then came the assurance. All along God had meant for the love of my earthly father to be a pattern of my heavenly Father and to show me the way to make connection with Him. Following this inner conviction came the sudden urge to act and the will to do it. To my surprise, and Mother's,

---

[3]Ibid., 27.

I rose from the pew and walked down the aisle to the front, joining a half dozen or so others.

At first, Dad did not see me as the group lined up in a semicircle around the altar. He spoke to us briefly about the step we were taking and was about to pray when he noticed me.

Full recognition flashed into his brown eyes; he knew instantly that my being there was significant. I was presenting the gift of myself, a first step of faith. The resistance had been broken.[4]

Catherine was nine years old when she took that step of faith. Her father nurtured her commitment to God and encouraged her to trust her heavenly Father. But it was her mother who showed Catherine how faith worked daily and who encouraged her to dream.

Catherine's mother, Leonora, was born in 1891 and was raised in North Carolina. When she was eighteen years of age, she volunteered to be a teacher for Dr. Edward O. Guerrant's mission, which was located in the Great Smoky Mountains of East Tennessee. Leonora's experiences with these mountain people formed the basis for Catherine's bestselling novel, *Christy*.

It was here that Leonora's creativity and resourcefulness blossomed. When the mission was in need of money, she took it upon herself to raise funds by appealing to a wealthy Knoxville businessman. She adorned herself in a new dress, put on an air of confidence, and convinced him that God's work was exciting. He, in turn, supplied the mission with enough food and money to last all winter.

It was also at the mission that Leonora met her future husband, John Wood. When she was nineteen years of age, they married, and for forty years they

---

4Ibid., 30.

faithfully served in the Presbyterian church. But times were not always comfortable and easy. Throughout Catherine's childhood, her parents struggled to make ends meet.

The little communities in which Catherine's father ministered were deeply affected by the Depression. This forced him to take several pay cuts out of an already lean salary. During those years, Catherine and her family lacked many luxuries, including a car. There was never enough money to buy new clothing or to put food on the table for the entire week.

So Catherine learned early on the sacrifices of ministry. She and her siblings often wore either hand-me-downs or clothing made for them by their mother. Her father on many occasions had to rely on the kindness of the grocer to provide what food was lacking each week. He would humbly ask him for an advance until he could pay.

Despite all these challenges, Leonora never thought they were poor. Her philosophy was to find the good in every circumstance. Her consistent, positive attitude and the actions that flowed from it had a tremendous impact on Catherine. She recalls this period of her life in this way:

> We children certainly did not enjoy those Depression years, yet no tinge of fear about lack of money ever clouded our home. It never seemed even to have entered Mother's head that we were living through a period of poverty. She went through each difficult day of the Depression as though she had some secret bank account to draw from when we were in need—and in a sense she did. But her real secret was an utterly confident inner attitude: always before her was the picture

of a healthy, fulfilled family.[5]

Leonora provided Catherine with many examples of faith in action. But none had more impact on her than her mother's pattern of giving. Out of utter scarcity Leonora was able to provide for the poorest of the poor. The lesson for Catherine was "no matter how little you have, you can always give some of it away. And when you can do that, you can't feel sorry for yourself, and you can scarcely consider yourself poor."[6]

Leonora's most shining example of charity was the work she did among the destitute of Mineral County, West Virginia. The vicinity called Radical Hill was home to more than five hundred desperate families. After surveying the area, Mrs. Wood offered her services to the welfare board and was immediately given a job to help improve living conditions there.

Her first task was to change the name of the vicinity from Radical Hill to Potomac Heights (the name of the river that flowed nearby). Second, she and her volunteers refurbished an old abandoned hotel and made it into a meeting place for all kinds of activities, including a Bible study and a childcare class given by herself.

At the height of this good work, the welfare board broke the news to Leonora that funding for her project had run out. With hardly a flinch, Mrs. Wood convinced the board to allow her work to continue without pay. This in itself was remarkable considering her own family's financial difficulties.

The director of the board, amazed by her tenacious and giving spirit, agreed to let her keep working. He also promised that he himself would help and would recruit others to join in the effort. So, through Leonora's inspiration, the work continued, and the community was renewed.

Catherine often marveled at her mother's many abilities. By the time she was twelve, she realized that her mother's great strength flowed from her relationship with God. It caused Catherine to wonder what it was like to know God in such an intimate way. Could her mother hear His voice? If so, what did it sound like? How did she know it was Him?

By fourteen years of age, Catherine was full of still more questions. Also, her heart began to awaken with daring, new thoughts. But she sincerely believed that the questions and desires that welled up inside of her were unanswerable and unattainable. As always, however, her mother intervened and inspired Catherine to dare to dream:

> You are the beloved children of the King. . . .
> Each of you is very special to Him, and He has important work for you to do in the world. It's up to you to find His dream for your life. And take warning, our King doesn't fool around with petty stuff. The sky is the limit![7]

Thus, by the time Catherine entered high school, with her mother's encouragement tucked away in her heart, she had formulated her first dream: to become an author. Shortly after this, a family friend spoke to Catherine about her own daughter's experiences at Agnes Scott College. She also told her that a man just right for her would soon come and take her away.

Accordingly, two more dreams took shape: to go to Agnes Scott College and to prepare herself for the

---

[7]Ibid., 43.

wonderful man who would come into her life. By her senior year of high school, these three dreams were the focus of Catherine's life. But the reality of the Depression soon began to snuff out her hope to attend Agnes Scott. She had already been accepted, but she fell hundreds of dollars short of being able to pay the tuition.

One night Leonora found her daughter in her bedroom crying over the situation. She said to her, "Catherine, I know it's right for you to go to college. . . . Every problem has a solution. Let's ask God to tell us how to bring this dream to reality."[8] What took place after this was a life-changing experience for Catherine.

Through her mother's prayers, Catherine was for the first time ushered into the presence of God. Unexpectedly, however, Catherine was also unmasked in the light of His presence. This was both a disturbing and freeing experience for her. Years later, she described this revolutionary moment:

> As we knelt there together, instinctively I knew that this was an important moment, one to be recorded in heaven. We were about to meet God in a more intimate way than at bedtime prayers or during grace before a meal, or in family prayers together in Dad's study, or even [than] in most of the prayers in church. Mother was admitting me to the inner sanctum of her prayer closet.
>
> In the silence, I quickly reviewed my relationship with this God with whom we were seeking an audience. At the age of nine I had given Him my life. . . .
>
> I had prayed many times since that encounter

---

[8]Ibid., 44.

with Him years before, but how real had these prayers been? The truth then struck me—most had been for selfish purposes. I had given so little of myself to Him. I had not really taken much part in Mother's work to transform Radical Hill to Potomac Heights. And with a sinking heart, I remembered all the times I had seen members of the church coming up the front walk, [and I would] flee up the back stairs to my room where I could be alone to read and not have to give myself to others in the sharing of their problems.

Scene after scene flashed across my mind's eye of the times I had resented my brother and sister. . . . As I thought of the many occasions when my parents had gone without something they needed so that we children could have new clothing, piano lessons, books, or sports equipment, I felt more unworthy than ever. And my going to college would call for yet more sacrifices from my parents.

I stole a look at my mother. She was praying intensely but soundlessly, with her lips moving. Then, closing my eyes, I silently prayed the most honest prayer of my life to that point. "Lord, I've been selfish. I've taken everything from You, from Your church, and from my parents and given little of myself in return. Forgive me for this, Lord. Perhaps I don't deserve to go to a college like Agnes Scott."

A sob deep in my throat made me pause. I knew what I now had to do. "And Lord, I turn this dream over to You. I give it up. It's in Your hands. You decide."

. . . I was learning that the price of a relationship with Him is a dropping of all our masks and pretense. We must come to Him with stark honesty "as we are"—or not at all. My honesty brought me relief; it washed away the guilt; it strengthened my faith."[9]

Not long after this, their petition was answered. Leonora received a letter from the federal government offering her a salary to write the history of the county. The money was more than enough to pay Catherine's tuition. Catherine stood in awe of the God of her mother—the God who forgave her selfish attitude and graciously supplied what she needed to attend college.

In the spring of Catherine's freshman year at Agnes Scott, another dream, her most precious one, came to the forefront. Her English professor had given an assignment in which the students were given a choice of several different authors to research. Catherine chose New Zealand short story writer Katherine Mansfield.

Catherine reveled in her research. It was an assignment of pure joy to her. When she turned her paper in, the teacher vehemently accused her of plagiarism. The style was so similar to Mansfield that she was convinced that this work was far beyond Catherine's ability to produce.

While this incident, with all its accusations and humiliation, broke Catherine's heart, she also gained confidence in her writing ability. She began to believe that just maybe her dream of becoming an author would someday be realized.

About this same time, Catherine began to hear rumors about a pastor at Westminster Presbyterian Church who was "a really good preacher . . . Scottish, and very handsome." She was intrigued and went to hear him. While she certainly thought he was good-looking, she was more moved by the things that he

[9]Ibid., 44–46.

said. He talked fervently about a present-day Jesus who was interested in every aspect of our lives.

This idea of a Jesus so involved in the daily affairs of life stupefied Catherine. It was a mystery to her, so much so that by the end of her sophomore year, she was feeling despondent. The distance she perceived between her and her God was almost too much for her to handle. Her journal entries reveal her state of mind at this time:

> I am awfully blue this morning for some unex-plainable reason. It must be that let-down feeling after all my exams. They were simply awful. I wonder if other people suffer as much as I do over them.
>
> I am tired all over. Mentally, physically, spiri-tually. I am lazy spiritually. I would like to know God really—not in the abstract. But I don't seem to want to badly enough to do anything much about it. I can't fathom myself. Perhaps some-day—but it's always someday.

Regular church attendance did not seem to lift her spirit either. Nevertheless, the Scottish preacher soon began to dominate Catherine's thoughts. His sermons haunted her day and night. One thing she quickly re-alized was, unlike him, she did not have that spiritual vitality or that inner peace that he so often spoke about. Her journal entries reveal her restlessness:

> I have come to a crisis in my life. It's very easy for me to see how people can lose their so-called religion when they have gotten enough education to make them think at all, particularly if their re-ligion is simply an inheritance or a habit. I'm afraid this is happening to me; I have had no real, vital religious experience. God does not seem real

to me. I believe in God now mostly because of people I know—a very few people . . . to whom religion is a vital, living thing.

I can't go on like this. I know there must be something to religion, else all of life would be meaningless. Sometimes it is to me. People hurry and bustle and strive, failing to see the beauty around them. Their eyes are on material consideration wholly. We die, and apparently it is all over. I wonder what I was born for after all. *I must know.*

Another entry says this:

Spring is so beautiful. All the trees are out now, a tangy fresh green. On the way to Decatur, I saw pink honeysuckle and lilacs, and the air is filled with the fragrance of wisteria. The earth is brown and wet and springy, full of the promise of better things—the hope of life and eternity.

Yet amid all this exquisite beauty, the world is also full of sordid, ugly things. My trip to the University of Georgia was so disheartening. The students there live what seems to me to be superficial and meaningless lives: drinking, always with cigarettes dangling from their lips, gossiping, and saying nothing when they do talk. None of them ever seems to study. Why do they go to college anyway?

There has got to be something more to life than this, some real purpose. What is my purpose? I don't think I've found it. I want my life to be so full. I want to be able to love and laugh and live and help others to the depth of my capacity.

Catherine was beginning to learn that she could not make it on her parents' faith. She was learning that faith, in order to be real, had to be her own. She was also beginning to realize that spiritual questions were answered only if they emerged from her own heart. So, for the first time with her own convictions, she finally inquired, "Where is God in all this?"

2

A Man Called Peter

God of our fathers in Whom we trust and by Whose guidance and grace this nation was born, bless the Senators of these United States at this important time in history and give them all things needful to the faithful discharge of their responsibilities.

We pray especially today for our President, and also for him who will preside over this chamber.

Give to them good health for the physical strains of their office, good judgment for the decisions they must make, wisdom beyond their own, and clear understanding for the problems of this difficult hour.

We thank Thee for their humble reliance upon Thee. May they go often to the throne of grace as we commend them both to Thy loving care and Thy guiding hand.

Through Jesus Christ our Lord, AMEN.

Peter Marshall
Inauguration Day
January 20, 1949[1]

---

[1]Catherine Marshall, *A Man Called Peter*, reprint. ed. (Grand Rapids, Mich.: Chosen Books, 1995), 12.

Peter Marshall was elected to the office of Chaplain of the Senate in 1947, and he faithfully served in that capacity until his death on January 25, 1949. Though it may not be readily apparent in the above prayer, Peter was a fiery preacher, full of conviction and fortitude. Many in Washington referred to him as the "conscience of the Senate."

But Peter's reputation spread far beyond the borders of Washington, D.C. A reporter from *The Chicago Sun-Times* once wrote an article about him entitled "A New Bite to Senate Prayers." The following is an excerpt from this telling piece:

> The least heeded of any of the millions of words uttered in the United States Senate had usually been those of the chaplain, who opens each session with prayer. But now some observers are beginning to urge Senators to get there early enough to hear these utterances, for the new chaplain, the Rev. Peter Marshall, pastor of the New York Avenue Presbyterian Church, avoids the usual platitudes and is handing out some tart advice to the lawmakers. . . .
>
> When Dr. Marshall prayerfully addressed his God, he first took pains to throw the stuffed shirt into the laundry bag. "We confess, our Father," he prayed one day in the chamber of the United States Senate, "that we know we need Thee, yet our swelled heads and our stubborn wills keep us trying to do without thee. Forgive us for making so many mountains out of molehills and for exaggerating both our own importance and the problems that confront us. . . ."[2]

---

[2]Leonard E. LeSourd, ed. *The Best of Catherine Marshall* (New York: Walker and Company, 1993), 58.

An editorial in *The Atlanta Journal* said:

> The Rev. Peter Marshall . . . a preacher who
> was a favorite among Atlantans a short time ago,
> awoke last Sunday morning to find his name, and
> excerpts from his sermon, on the front page of
> practically every newspaper in the nation. . . .
>
> A native of Scotland . . . he combines with deep
> religious sincerity an arresting pulpit personality
> and holds his hearers enthralled by the almost
> dramatic forcefulness of his delivery. . . .
>
> He won more than local popularity during his
> Atlanta pastorate and now, in Washington, has
> made his name one of nationwide significance.
> The opportunity to serve that has thus come to the
> Rev. Peter Marshall at an early age is one enjoyed
> by few men. . . .[3]

It might be natural to think that a young minister
who preached and prayed with such power and conviction would have had from boyhood a heart for the
ministry. But it was not that way with Peter Marshall.
As a child, his first great love was the sea. His ultimate desire was to become an admiral in the British
Navy.

However, God had in mind for Peter a different
"sea"—the sea of humanity. His desire was for Peter
to lead people to the living waters—to the springs of
eternal life. Through a series of events in Peter's
young adult life, he finally came to accept the Chief's
orders.

Peter Marshall was born in Coatbridge, Scotland,
in 1902. His father, whom he adored, died when Peter
was only four years old. A few years later, his mother
remarried. At that point, young Peter, who was deeply

---

[3]*A Man Called Peter*, 138–139.

opposed to his mother's remarriage, was thrown into emotional turmoil. He longed to escape to the inviting and mysterious waters of the sea.

Coatbridge was situated roughly nine miles from the ocean and the navy shipyards. Frequent trips to this area fueled Peter's dream of becoming a Navy admiral. Undoubtedly, dissatisfaction with his homelife also nurtured his obsession with the great waters. For hours he would read novels about the sea and fantasize about journeys on navy ships.

At fourteen years of age, Peter's dream came true when he signed on with the British Navy. But his navy career lasted only two short days. The problem was that the navy signed boys who were fifteen years and nine months or older. When it was discovered that he was only fourteen, he was forced to leave.

To add to this disappointment, his parents refused to give him consent to join at such a young age. Refusing to give up on his dream, however, Peter decided to take a job and to go to technical school in order to prepare himself for the day when he could reapply to the navy. He studied mechanical engineering, Morse code, and trigonometry.

At twenty-one years of age, he took a job as a machinist at Stewarts and Lloyds Imperial Tube Works. Though his weekly salary was barely enough to care for his needs while at home, he decided to strike out on his own.

His mother knew all too well that thirty-eight shillings a week was not enough to pay for room, board, and schooling. Nevertheless, she helped him pack, prayed for him, and committed him to God's care. Shortly after this, Peter's boss called him into the office. Peter feared he was about to be laid off; but, instead, he was given a promotion and double the pay.

Through his mother's prayers, God met him at his point of need. This left a lasting impression on Peter.

Besides work and school, Peter was deeply involved in his church and in various sporting activities. The group of friends he ran with consistently influenced him toward the things of God. Eric Liddell, Scotland's greatest and best-known athlete, also had a tremendous influence on Peter. In many ways, Peter modeled Eric's method of Christian witness.

Though young Marshall was not yet aware of it, God was using these influences to carefully shape his destiny. Through many twisting circumstances, Peter slowly began to get the message.

For example, one starless night, after working in a nearby English village, Peter decided to take a short cut home. The particular wasteland in which he was walking had in it a deep limestone quarry. As he was walking, Peter heard a loud voice call out his name. He asked who it was but got no response. As he continued to walk, he heard the voice again. At that moment Peter stumbled and fell. When he felt the ground around him, he realized he was at the edge of the quarry.

Through a still, small voice, God had warned Peter of near disaster. This was the beginning point of the time in which God convinced Peter that He had a purpose for his life.

Peter still thought the navy was in his future. But then a missionary came to speak to the young people in the Buchanan Street Kirk. Peter was so moved by his message that he was convinced God was calling him into full-time Christian ministry. "I have determined," he said, "to give my life to God for him to use me wherever he wants me."

Not long after this, his cousin, who had emigrated

to the United States, came back to Scotland for a visit. He encouraged Peter to come to America and build his ministry. Peter was very reluctant to go. However, after three weeks of prayer and deep soul-searching, Peter knew that "the Chief" was giving him his marching orders. Years later, in 1933, in a sermon entitled "Under Sealed Orders," Peter spoke of his God-directed journey to the United States. The following is an excerpt from this extraordinary sermon:

> I do not know what picture the phrase "under sealed orders" suggests to you. In these terrible times, it may have several connotations. . . .
>
> To me, it recalls very vividly a scene from the First World War, when I was a little boy, spending vacations at a Scottish seaport.
>
> I saw a gray destroyer slipping hurriedly from port in response to urgent orders. . . . I watched the crew hurry their preparations for sailing, watched them cast off the mooring hawsers. . . .
>
> [I] saw the sleek ship get under way, as she rose to meet the lazy ground swell of a summer evening . . . with her Morse lamp winking on the control bridge aft. . . .
>
> [I] watched her until she was lost in the mist of the North Sea. She was a mystery vessel. She had sailed "under sealed orders." Not even her officers knew her destination or the point of rendezvous.
>
> So, in like manner, all the pioneers of faith have gone out—and all the explorers: Abraham of old, Columbus, the Cabots, Magellan, Balboa, John Smith, Peary, MacMillan, Scott, Lindbergh, Byrd.
>
> They all went out in faith, not knowing what lay ahead. Sometimes this going out in obedience to God's command is more dramatic than at other

times . . . sometimes more spectacular . . . sometimes more brave . . . but always it is a venture
into the unknown.

I know something of what it means to go out
like that for I have experienced it in my own life.
Well do I remember on the 19th of March, 1927,
standing on the aft deck of the Cameronia, watching with strangely moist eyes, the purple hills of
the Mull of Kintyre sinking beneath the screw-
thrashed waters of the Atlantic, when every turn
of the propeller was driving me farther from the
land of my birth—from all I knew and loved. . . .

I was coming to the United States to enter the
ministry, because I believed, with all my heart,
that those were my orders from my Chief. But I
did not know how or when or where. I could not
foresee the wonderful way in which God would
open doors of opportunity.

I could never have imagined the romantic,
thrilling way in which God was to arrange my life
. . . order my ways, guide my steps, provide for all
my needs, give me wonderful friends, generous
helpers until, at last, I would achieve His plan for
me, and be ordained a minister of the Gospel. . . .[4]

Once he touched American soil, Peter's life took off
like a whirlwind. He arrived in America on April 5,
1927. He took a job as a manual laborer for a New Jer-
sey utility where he worked ten long hours a day.
Some friends then encouraged him to go to Birmingham, Alabama. There he took a job as a proofreader
for the *Birmingham News* and became a layleader in
a Presbyterian church. The church sponsored him into
Columbia Seminary where his gift of preaching developed rapidly.

---

[4]Ibid., 34–36.

His first pastorate was at Covington Presbyterian Church in Birmingham. Then, the struggling Westminster Presbyterian Church in Atlanta called him to come to the pastorate. Under Peter's leadership, Westminster was revitalized, and people from all over Atlanta were drawn to it, including those from Agnes Scott College.

As was alluded to in the previous chapter, Catherine was one of those from Agnes Scott who was captivated by the preaching of this Scottish minister. His sermons often put her on a spiritual and emotional roller coaster—exciting, and yet unsettling at times. But it was not long before the man behind the message started to appeal to her.

In the beginning she reasoned that her attraction to him was silly girlish immaturity. She once commented in her journal, "I don't know what's the matter with me. Perhaps I'm simply in a romantic frame of mind these days, but that man Peter Marshall does something to me! I would give anything I own to meet him." In an attempt to rid her mind of these "school girl" romantic thoughts, Catherine tried to stay away from Westminster. But she could not. It was as if a magnet was luring her back time and again. Soon she found herself pouring over books about Scottish history. She wanted to learn everything she could about Peter's birthplace.

But Catherine was not the only one under the spell of infatuation. Mr. Marshall himself had given Catherine a second look on several occasions. One of her journal entries says this:

> Went to Sunday school and church at Westminster. After Peter had made his talk, he said he didn't know everyone in the class and couldn't we

have a social to get acquainted? He said he wanted to meet some of us before all of us had a chance to get married. And then the funny part of it was that he actually blushed!

I had the strange and giddy feeling today that it was this particular morning that Mr. Marshall really noticed me for the first time. I could tell by the way he looked and smiled at me. It must have been my new blue hat, which was very becoming. . . .

It was obvious to Catherine that Peter had an eye on her. He often singled her out in the pew when he was preaching, and on several occasions he had his secretary ask her if he could drive her back to school. But, rather than making her happy, all of this added to the spiritual and emotional chaos Catherine was experiencing at this time.

She was unsure of herself, she was unsettled in her relationship with God, and now she was completely undone by the presence of Peter Marshall in her life. Many of the journal entries she made throughout her junior year at Agnes Scott reveal her tumultuous state of mind. The following are a few excerpts:

There are several reasons why I'm attracted to Peter. For one thing, he has so much poetry in his soul. There is such a kinship between poetry and religion. They both try to see into the heart of things.

One of the reasons I could never fall in love with Fred [a young man she had recently stopped dating] is that he has no appreciation for the beautiful. But then added to that, Peter combines an inheritance of the best of the European tradition with an acquisition of the best of the American. He has such a capacity for affection and tenderness, such a luscious sense of humor sprinkled with an earthy roguishness.

Why must the embodiment of all my ideal be twelve years older than I and as remote as the South Pole? . . .

Tonight I feel compelled to write until my hand is tired and exhausted. I am restless and unhappy these days because I am neither right with myself nor right with God. Why this dissatisfaction with myself? I am driven on and on by an overwhelming sense of some destiny, of some task to be done which I must do. I can never be peaceful and happy and enjoy life until I learn why I am here and where I am going.

It is as if my soul is frozen and hard, and when there comes some mellow influence which melts it, my soul strains against these walls like a turbulent mountain stream whose course has been newly freed from encumbering rubbish. And I don't think it too dramatic to say that my life is just as barren and dry as the rocky stream-bed, parched through being deprived of the life-giving water.

I am tired of knowing and not doing, tired of thinking and not being. I despise myself because I am simply lazy in my religion. It is easier not to bother. Yet I know that I can never find God by not bothering. . . .

The more I hear [Peter] talk, the more I realize we have the same ideas and ideals—we like the same things. . . . How I wish I could tell him all the sleep he has made me lose. . . . Dreaming this way about Peter is the most foolish thing that has ever happened to me.

To this point, Peter and Catherine had only known

each other in a casual way. They would occasionally see each other at church functions or in the vestibule after church services. But on May 3, 1935, a turning point came in their relationship when they attended a Prohibition rally at a local schoolhouse. Peter and another student from Emory University were scheduled to speak at the event.

On the drive back home, Peter held Catherine's hand the entire way. He explained to her that for a long time he had wanted to talk with her but never got the chance. He asked her if she would like to go bowling with him sometime, to which she said yes, and then said good-night.

Catherine was on top of the world. Yet a week went by, and there was no call from Peter. During that time, they saw each other at church functions, and he was attentive toward her. He even drove her back to college. But still there was no call. Finally, on May 12, he asked her for a date, and they were together until late that evening.

Afterward, Peter promised to get in touch with her later that week. But again there was no call. Summer vacation came, and Catherine went back home to West Virginia, disgusted. She could not understand how Peter could adore her in person but deprive her of the assurance she needed by not calling her.

Peter promised to write Catherine during summer vacation, and he did. The first letter arrived on June 17, 1935. However, much to Catherine's surprise and shock, the letter was impersonal and remote. Not long after this, he sent her a postcard from Scotland that was even more dispassionate. Catherine was heartbroken. She determined to stay away from Westminster Church and Peter Marshall when she returned to Agnes Scott for her senior year. When the fall semester began, she poured herself into her studies and extracurricular activities. Even so, as hard as she tried to occupy herself with other things, she could not get Peter off her mind.

On October 20 she went to Westminster. In her journal, Catherine recorded what took place on their first meeting since the previous spring and how it led to further involvement with each other:

> Went to church at Westminster, but got there after 11 A.M. and had to sit in the vestibule and listen to Peter through the loudspeaker. I had planned not to speak to him afterward, but suddenly changed my mind. He pumped my hand and commented that this was the first time I had been here this year. So he had noticed my absence! He promised to get in touch with me. I shan't hold my breath until he does.
>
> Gossip continues about the different women Peter goes out with. I don't think he plays around, but being a tender and affectionate person, succumbs for the moment and gives women the wrong impression. The reason he has never gotten married is that none of us has ever really come up to his ideal. . . .
>
> I was invited to have dinner with Peter at the Robinsons, to which he was quite late. Right away he brought up the past spring. Had I remembered it? We ended up looking at his pictures of Scotland, drinking tea, talking. He said he would call me, but I am skeptical. And so Peter once more invades my smug and fortified existence.

The same pattern continued in their relationship. Peter was attentive and warm when at church and at church functions but rarely called her on campus. Then a crucial turning point came in their relationship on May 3, 1936. Catherine was asked to review a book for the Sunday afternoon fellowship hour. She chose the book *Prayer* by Dr. O. Hallesby.

When the Sunday arrived on which she was to give her speech, Catherine was nervous to the point of being ill. She was well-prepared to give the talk, but the thought of Peter being in the audience was overwhelming. He was there in the front, right in her view.

"We tend to be superficial in our prayers," she began. "Most of us think of God as a kind of Santa Claus who waits to hear our requests. What He really wants to hear are the hungers of our heart and our confessions of deception and dishonesty."[5]

As she spoke, her nervousness dissipated, and the peace and power of God descended on her. Everyone who attended the review was touched by her presentation and impressed by her speaking ability. Peter was especially moved. Nevertheless, Catherine could not stay for the evening service because of the churning in her stomach.

The next day, while having lunch with his secretary, Ruby Calamine, Peter was silent. He asked her why every girl he ever cared about had to leave town. He knew that Catherine was going to graduate that year and move back to West Virginia. Ruby, knowing of their growing relationship, assured him that he could do something about it this time.

That afternoon Peter went to Agnes Scott to visit Catherine in the infirmary. When she got the call, she was flabbergasted. No man had ever been allowed into the infirmary before, and she wondered how he managed to wriggle himself in. However, as touched as she was by his concern, Catherine encouraged him not to

---

[5]*Meeting God at Every Turn*, 72.

come see her, but that she would go to meet him.

Not long after this incident, she recorded the following in her journal:

> Peter was terribly solicitous about my illness. . . . I believe now he wants to be serious. . . . I think Peter is in love with me! Tonight we went to a play. Afterward on the front porch he kissed me again and again. . . . Tonight we talked until three in the morning and he proposed. . . .

This was the big moment she had been waiting for—a proposal from the man of her dreams. But she hesitated. Three years before, in her freshman year, Catherine had asked the question, "Where is God in all this?" Through her college career she slowly began to realize that God is active in every aspect of human affairs, even romance.

So Catherine needed to make sure that this move was indeed God's will for her life and not something that she was just asking God to bless. Peter and Catherine prayed both together and separately about marriage. Soon she was convinced that from the beginning God had his hand on their relationship.

She accepted his proposal, and they were married by her father on November 4, 1936, in Keyser, West Virginia. Two of Catherine's three lifelong dreams had come to pass: she attended Agnes Scott College and met the man who swept her off her feet. Now they would live together to a ripe old age, happily ever after. Or so she thought.

3

The School of Green Pastures

Peter and Catherine spent their wedding night at a hotel in Washington, D.C. The next morning Mr. Marshall had a meeting with the pastoral staff at the old New York Avenue Presbyterian Church. Peter had told Catherine about this meeting several weeks before their wedding; but he was still uncomfortable about leaving his new wife on their honeymoon.

Once the meeting was underway, Catherine came to join them. Being quite nervous, she prayed that she would do nothing to embarrass her new husband. The committee announced to both of them that they wanted Peter to take over the pastorate. But, much to their disappointment, he quickly turned down the call.

The reason for this was twofold. First, he felt his work was not yet finished in Atlanta. The Lord was opening doors for him to minister in ways that convinced him God wanted him to stay in Georgia. Secondly, he felt he was not yet ready to take on such an enormous responsibility.

When they returned to Atlanta, Peter and Catherine settled down into the cottage he had picked out during their engagement. Peter vigorously continued his work at Westminster while Catherine stayed at home, content and happy in her new role. She spent a majority of her time working on the garden, which brought her great satisfaction and pleasure. Life, for the most part, was calm and peaceful.

Peter loved to preach. He would rather be in a pulpit than anywhere else. Out-of-town speaking engagements were especially alluring to him. But when he was away, he was always eager to get back home to his wife. Just a few months after they were married, while away on his first speaking engagement since the wedding, he wrote Catherine a short letter:

> My dearest,
>   Since getting down here I have longed to get busy in the garden and plant flowers, longed almost poignantly for the things I left behind. I mean, apart from my longing for you and to be with you—everything we have seems to mean so much to me now. . . . This is the first time we have been separated for so long since our wedding, except for your trip home. Only three more days. . . . I'll be so glad to get back on Friday night. . . . Expect me about 11 or earlier, if I can get away. . . .[1]

Peter loved having his wife at home. In fact, he firmly believed that God's plan for the married woman was to stay at home and take care of her family. He did not hide his views from the public, but openly declared what he believed the Scriptures taught about the marriage relationship. So candid was he about his

---

[1] *A Man Called Peter*, 151.

beliefs on this subject that *The Washington Post* ran a feature article about them:

MARRIAGE A FULL-TIME JOB FOR ANY WOMAN, ASSERTS PASTOR

Dr. Marshall Sees Menace in Career Wives. Believes Their Ambition Threatens Home Life. Grants Exceptions for Economic Necessity.

A girl who is not willing to give up her name, her career, her own selfish ambitions, for her husband's sake had better stay out of marriage, for she will not create a successful, happy home. This is the theory of Dr. Peter Marshall . . . who bases his opinion on his wide experience in helping young people solve their problems.

"Many girls today are unwilling to make marriage a full-time job," said Dr. Marshall. "They prefer a career to a home or try to mix both. The idea of a woman's taking time out from business to start a family is not only absurd, but it is breaking down the fundamental ideals of family life.

"Of course, there are many exceptions, and I am not referring to those married women who are forced by economic necessity to continue working. . . ."

Ambition, desire for luxuries, and boredom with domestic life are many married women's incentives for jobs or careers, Dr. Marshall believes. Such an attitude, plus economic independence, accounts for many unhappy homes and eventually leads to divorce, he maintains. . . .

Woman's greatest chance for making marriage a success depends upon her willingness to lose her life in that of her husband, Dr. Marshall holds. He means that the wife's interests must be those of her husband; she must be willing to make little sacrifices to help him along the way. . . .

"Despite the fact that one marriage in every six in this country ends in divorce, young people want to make their marriages succeed, and they want it desperately. I can testify to the deep sincerity of purpose in the hearts of the young men and women who speak to me about being married. Yet, aware of the pitfalls and dangers that lie ahead in modern marriages and armed with sincerity of purpose, still many of them fail. From this, one must conclude that the average modern view of marriage must be wrong, and that the old-fashioned idea of marriage must be the soundest after all."[2]

Catherine heartily supported her husband's views on the married woman and gladly submitted to them. Much like her experience with her father, she felt safe and secure in Peter's presence. She depended on him for everything, and he welcomed her vulnerability.

However, despite his rather strict beliefs about marriage, he always treated her like an equal and even eagerly accepted her thoughts concerning life decisions. A case in point was the issue concerning the call to go to Washington.

The invitation to take the pastorate at New York Avenue Presbyterian Church came once again. This time Peter and Catherine beseeched the Lord more intensely about it. They decided to keep their hearts open to God's will, whatever it may be. Eventually, the two of them were convinced that God was calling Peter to go to Washington, D.C.

So on October 3, 1937, when Peter was thirty-five and Catherine was twenty-three, he began his min-

---

[2]*The Washington Post*, Dec. 23, 1938, as quoted in *A Man Called Peter*, 157–158.

istry there. At first Peter was quite tentative in his new role, not sure how to address the capital city crowd. Everyone from the president to the common person attended his services.

When he realized, however, that the rich and the powerful have deep spiritual needs like everyone else, Peter let go of his conservatism and preached what God put on his heart. In a matter of weeks, the sanctuary was filled to capacity. Even in the diverse setting of Washington, D.C., Peter was able to make God a reality to everyone who heard his sermons.

Needless to say, Peter's immense popularity had a tremendous impact on Catherine's daily life. Like her husband, though, she determined to live up to this new calling. She prayed and asked God to help her fit into her new role. God answered by sending her women who taught her how to dress, how to serve, and how to live out the New York Avenue traditions, which dated back to the time of Thomas Jefferson.

It wasn't long before Catherine felt comfortable in her position. She was proud of her husband and content with herself. But she often pushed beyond her physical capabilities, not eating enough or sleeping enough to keep up with her busy schedule. She was in desperate need of rest in order to keep up with the changes that lay ahead.

On Sunday, January 21, 1940, at 8:53 in the morning, Peter John Marshall was born. His father, who nicknamed him "Wee Peter," was on top of the world. The entire congregation was ecstatic about the new addition and affectionately referred to him as "Re-Pete." As for Catherine, her happiness was now complete.

However, her bliss was interrupted when, three years after Peter John was born, in 1943, her health took a mighty tumble. She was diagnosed with tuberculosis and ordered to stay in bed for at least three to four months. What a blow! *Who will look after the house and take care of Peter John?* she wondered.

As it turned out, a full-time nurse was needed to care for Catherine because she could not even lift her arm to feed herself. She was allowed to get up only to go to the bathroom. Her mother and a succession of nannies, maids, and governors looked after Peter John. It was an especially desperate time for Catherine and a difficult one for her entire family.

She did not realize it at first, but God was about to complete the spiritual training begun several years earlier when Catherine was a student at Agnes Scott. There she went through a period of uncertainty about herself and about God. He would now use this time to train her as a disciple and to prepare her for further changes ahead.

Catherine came to refer to this down time as the "Green Pastures" classroom. The verse in Psalm 23, "He maketh me to lie down in green pastures," came alive to her in this experience. She realized that God allowed this illness—made her to lie down—in order to get her full attention.

What she did not know at the time was that this journey to healing, both physical and spiritual, was to last not three or four months but more than two years. In this period of complete bed rest, the Lord took Catherine through four phases of instruction. The things she learned during this time utterly transformed her and shaped the outcome of the rest of her life.

Her first task was (to become more deeply and intimately acquainted with the Lord.) She accomplished this by consistently pouring over the Scriptures. She was particularly interested in Christ's miracles of healing, especially as they related to the faith of those who were healed. Those who received healing took Christ at His Word.

In other words, she learned that faith is needed in order to be healed. This created a great dilemma for Catherine. She had faith in Christ, but she was not healed. Month after month went by, and still there was no change in her condition.

Then one day Mrs. Marshall made what she considered to be an eye-opening discovery. She later recounted this event:

> And had not God promised us that His Word "would never return unto Him void"? Then surely our claiming with faith any one of these promises for ourselves was the way to healing. Yet it did not work the way I expected . . . then what was the way to real faith? Subsequently I would be shown the difference between the *Logos*, one of the two Greek nouns used for God's written word in Scripture, and the *Rhea*. The latter is that part of the *Logos* to which the Holy Spirit points us personally, which He illuminates and brings to life for us in our particular situation.
>
> For instance, out of all the Old Testament *Logos*, the Spirit had pointed out to me and emblazoned into my consciousness, nine words from the second verse of Psalm 23: "He maketh me to lie down in green pastures." Those nine words were His *rhea* spoken directly by the Lord himself to me. . . .
>
> The point is that Jesus will not allow us to use Scripture as only an historical document or as a set of automatic rules. To do so is to ignore the risen, living Lord standing there just beside us at any given moment. . . . So our Lord stands senti-

nel over His Book to show us that we can use His word in Scripture with real power only as He himself energizes it and speaks to us personally through it.[3]

So Catherine accepted Christ's personal word to her, which was not immediate healing, but continued learning. In her second phase of instruction, she learned *to become completely transparent before Him.* As painful as it was, she allowed Christ's light to shine on the darkest areas of her being. A journal entry reveals her startled reaction to His discoveries:

> This morning came a disturbing thought. For years I have yearned for a free time away from household duties, for a quiet time—alone, undisturbed. I was never able to obtain it—until I went to bed sick last March. *Could I have wanted to be rid of the burdens of daily living so much that I had a deep unconscious desire for illness as an escape—once I had made the difficult adjustment to bed rest—from them?* In this sense, therefore, my illness has been satisfying. I have had all the time I wanted for quiet communication with the Lord, and others have carried my burdens for me.
>
> The Lord has asked me the direct question, "Do you want to be well?" In other words, "Are you ready to face up to life, to assume the responsibilities of a normal person?"
>
> I can see that He wants me to be well. He wants to cure me. He wants my answer to be "yes." Therefore, to say "no" would be to frustrate His will.
>
> One part of me wants to be well, but another part of me is still hugging the bed, still exceed-

---

[3]*Meeting God at Every Turn*, 88–90.

ingly loathed to part with it. I have given Him my will in the matter, though, and asked Him to heal this schism in me, to make me want His will totally and to give me joy in it.[4]

Catherine was shocked to discover that there could be a part of her that did not want to be healed. She thought there was nothing she wanted more; especially since, as each passing month brought no change in her condition, she was sinking deeper and deeper into despair.

The third stage in her teaching came in the summer of 1944, when she and her family went to Cape Cod. The Lord impressed on her that she was *to learn all there was to know about the Holy Spirit.* Once again, Catherine poured over the Scriptures and discovered the multifaceted nature of the Holy Spirit. She described her experience in this way:

All summer I gave a minimum of an hour a day to this. . . . Morning by morning revealed new truths—new to me at least. . . . The messages kept piling up. Though not a one of us can recognize Jesus as who He really is until the Spirit reveals this to us, nonetheless, the fullness of the Holy Spirit is not something that happens automatically at conversion. His coming to us and living within us is a gift, the best gift the Father can give us. But the Father always waits on our volition. Jesus told us that we have to desire this gift of gifts, ask for it—ask for Him.[5]

At this point, Catherine sensed that the Lord was calling her to a deeper level of obedience. Thus, the

---

[4]Ibid., 91.
[5]Ibid., 94.

fourth stage of her instruction was *to learn to be stead-fastly obedient.* In response, she uttered this prayer:

> Lord, from this moment I promise that I'll try to do whatever You tell me in order to get well, insofar as You'll make clear to me what Your wishes are. I'm weak, and many times I'll probably want to renege on this. But Lord, you'll have to help me with that, too.

She recorded this prayer in her journal and dated it. Now Catherine was beginning to feel that maybe her long journey was coming to an end. Since she had grown so much spiritually, she thought physical health was possibly just around the corner. And there was some physical improvement, which gave her a glint of hope.

But then something unexpected happened. Catherine was hit with an emotional setback, a time when she was plagued with feelings of unworthiness. She feared that Peter no longer desired her or needed her as a wife. She felt unattractive and helpless.

However, the Lord quickly revealed to her that this was a spiritual attack and gave her specific instructions on how to handle it. A journal entry records her insights:

> There is fear in me that someone else will usurp my place in Peter's heart. I have often tried to make myself believe that it is fear for Peter, his reputation, his ministry and his spiritual welfare. But is it really? Isn't it simply fear for myself? I have prayed about this over and over and get temporary peace, but then soon the same old fears engulf me again. Today I prayed that God would show me how to pray about it, that He would show me the lever by which I could lift it up to Him.

Within a matter of minutes, this verse clearly came to me: "Resist not evil." In other words, the way to win out when I feel evil [is] at work in my life and in the lives of those I love, is not to fight it in the ordinary sense, but to give over completely into the Father's hands those I love, knowing that I am helpless to cope with evil, but that "He is able."

I am to let my loved ones walk on into the lion's den; let evil come on in any guise it chooses—God will shut the lion's mouths. God will surround the one given over to Him with a league of His angels. If I think no evil thoughts, God will not let me be hurt, because I am willing to trust Him.

It is clear that Catherine was learning to be sensitive to the Holy Spirit's voice and to obey His specific instructions. She felt she was learning this lesson well. And what followed for her was consistent joy and peace in His presence.

Catherine returned to Washington with great anticipation for her next doctor's visit. But the X-rays revealed no significant change in her condition. Mrs. Marshall was completely dejected. So she went to Virginia to stay with her parents for two weeks. What else, she wondered, could she possibly do to get well?

There was only one thing left for her to do: offer up a prayer of relinquishment.

"Lord," she said, "I understand no part of this, but if You want me to be an invalid for the rest of my life—well, it's up to You. I place myself in Your hands, for better or for worse. I ask only to serve You."

As it turns out, this is exactly what the Lord was waiting for. Catherine never would have been willing (to give herself completely over to the lordship of Christ had she not gone through this two-year illness). Her training, for now, was complete. She had surrendered herself, and the Lord was pleased. On top of this incredible adventure, the Lord blessed Catherine with a vision of himself. Here is her account of the amazing event:

In the middle of the night I was awakened. The room was in total darkness. Instantly sensing something alive, electric in the room, I sat bolt upright in bed. Past all credible belief, suddenly, unaccountably, Christ was there, in Person, standing by the right side of my bed. I could see nothing but a deep, velvety blackness around me, but the bedroom was filled with an intensity of power, as if the Dynamo of the universe were there. Every nerve in my body tingled with it, as with a shock of electricity. I knew that Jesus was smiling at me tenderly, lovingly, whimsically—as though a trifle amused at my too-intense seriousness about myself. His attitude seemed to say, "Relax! There's not a thing wrong here that I can't take care of."

His personality held an amazing meld I had never before met in any one person: warmhearted compassion and the light touch, yet unmistakable authority and kingliness. Instantly, my heart wanted to bow before Him in abject adoration.

Would He speak to me? I waited in awe for Him to say something momentous, to give me my marching orders. "Go," He said in reply to my unspoken question. "Go, and tell your mother. That's easy enough, isn't it?"

Jesus said nothing more. He had told me what to do. At that moment I understood as never before the totality of His respect for the free will He has given us and the fact that He will never violate it. His attitude said, "The decision is entirely yours."

But I also learned at that moment the life-and-death importance of obedience. There was the feeling that my future hung on my decision. So brushing aside any inconsequential thoughts of Mother's reaction, with resolution I told Him, "I'll do it if it kills me"—and swung my legs over the side of the bed."[6]

In obedience, Catherine told her mother about the entire experience. When she returned to Washington, she went in for her routine chest X-ray. For the first time in more than two years, there was a vast improvement. Within six months of Christ's visitation, Mrs. Marshall was completely well.

Catherine emerged from her bed and from the "school of green pastures" with a new sense of the wonder of Christ. Through those months filled with valleys of disappointment and fires of purification, He had led her on the path of true discipleship. The vital lessons she learned armed her with ample spiritual strength to face life's challenges.

As it turns out, the first challenge was just around the corner. On January 25, 1949, at about 3:30 A.M., Peter woke Catherine complaining of severe chest pains. She immediately called an ambulance, which came and took him to the hospital. Peter's last words to her before he was taken away were, "Darling, I'll see you in the morning." At 8:25 A.M., the doctor phoned Catherine to inform her that Peter was dead. *How could this be?* she thought. Catherine immediately felt as if she had entered into a dream world.

When she went to see him in the hospital room, she

[6]Ibid., 98–99.

was met by a familiar Presence. She described this moving experience with these words:

> As I opened the door and stepped inside the small room, there was the instantaneous awareness that I was not alone. Yet the man I loved was not in the still form on the bed. Though I did not understand it then and cannot explain it now, I knew that Peter was near and alive. And beside him was another Presence of transcendent glory, the Lord he had served through long years—years stretching back to his young manhood in Scotland.
>
> Having already experienced that glory, how could I ever again doubt the fact of immortality? In a deep and intuitive way, beyond argument or intellectual process, deeper than tears, transcending words, came the knowledge that human life does not end in six feet of earth.
>
> Yet the realization of the splendor was not to last. In that still hospital room, at a precise moment, the two vied presences withdrew. Suddenly I saw Death stripped bare, in all its ugliness. With very human eyes I saw it: the fact of the man so dear to me. There's nothing pretty about death. Those who sentimentalize it, lie. Carbon dioxide escaping from the sagging jaw. The limp hands. The coldness and white, white pallor of flesh.

Suddenly Peter's last words to her took on new significance. She would see him again in the Morning, when the New Day dawned on the other side, where there were no more tears or mourning or darkness or pain. But, for now, she was to continue in the land of this existence—without him. The task seemed almost unbearable.

Catherine turned and left the room. She felt as if she was in a nightmare and all she had to do was wake up and it would be over. She did not know what her future held, but, thanks to the "School of Green Pastures" experience, she knew the One who held her future. Still—would knowledge of Him be enough for her?

4

Goodness and Mercy Shall Follow. . . .

For months Catherine groped around in the darkness trying to make some sense of her loss. She was numb for days, going through the motions of tending to the details of Peter's funeral service. Eight days after the funeral, the numbness wore off, and reality set in. Peter was gone. Now Mrs. Marshall was going to have to face life without him.

Death had never come so close to her. As a child, whenever death would remotely cross her path, Catherine would subconsciously deny it as part of the human experience. She would avoid funerals and all the solemn events affiliated with them. She thought if she avoided them, she would not have to deal with the emotional pain associated with them.

Peter sensed this attitude in her and on one occasion confronted her about it: "Get a piece of paper, Catherine," he told her. "There are some facts you must have down for ready reference in case anything should happen to me."

Everything in Catherine rebelled against this

thought. "I'll put this stuff down to humor you. But I can't stand to hear you talk that way. Nothing is going to happen to you. Don't be foolish. . . ."[1]

"You act," Peter said to her calmly, "as if death can be avoided by willing it away." Unconsciously, this is exactly what Catherine thought.

As a result, she was not in the least prepared for widowhood. Besides this, she was only thirty-four years old, and her son was only nine. Catherine openly confessed her inability to cope with this problem:

> In many ways, I was still a little girl. I had adored and leaned on my husband. Like many a sheltered woman who has married young, I had never once figured out an income tax blank, had a car inspected, consulted a lawyer, or tried to read an insurance policy. Railroad timetables and place schedules were enigmas to me. My household checking account rarely balanced. I had never invested any money; I had been driving a car for only three months. . . . The adjustment that faced me, therefore, posed a challenge in every way in which a woman can be challenged.[2]

So, as always, Catherine turned to her Lord. He gave her no concrete answers, but only the assurance that He would be her comfort. In one of her writings she spoke about this divine comfort with gleaming confidence:

> Peter Marshall's death from a heart attack at forty-six was a devastating blow. "Why?" I asked the Lord. "Why take a man who loves You so

---

[1]Catherine Marshall, *To Live Again*, reprint. ed. (Grand Rapids, Mich.: Chosen Books, 1996), 15.
[2]Ibid., 15–16.

much, who is in the prime time of life, whose impact on people for You is so great?" In the midst of grief, I had a million whys.

Not one of them was answered. Instead, into my anguished emotions there crept one morning a strange, all-pervading peace. Through and around me flowed love as I had never before experienced it. It was as if Someone who loved me very much were wrapping me round and round with His infinite care and protection.

I knelt there marveling at what was happening. I had done nothing, said nothing, to bring it about. I understood no more than before the reason for my young husband's death. I only knew that in some way that transcended reason, it was deeply and eternally all right. Into my midst came a verse from the Bible, "Underneath are the everlasting arms." That described what I was feeling. I opened my New Testament and found these strength-imparting words:

"So, up with your listless hands! Strengthen your weak knees. And make straight paths for your feet to walk in" (Hebrews 12:11–12, MOF-FATT).[3]

And Catherine did just that. As she had walked through her two-year illness learning to depend on the Lord every step of the way, so did she take His hand through the trials of grief. The first thing the Lord gave Catherine was comfort through His Word. As she studied the Scriptures, she found that they were shot through with references to the fatherless and the widow.

She learned that many of the promises of comfort

[3]Catherine Marshall, *Light in My Darkest Night* (Grand Rapids, Mich.: Chosen Books, 1989), 19–20.

and blessing were directed especially to them. She also saw that God's way to comfort is "not to whittle down the problem but to build up our ability to cope with it."[4] So she drew strength from many of the victory themes in the Bible.

Next, Catherine learned to accept God's comfort from His people. However, she discovered that comfort does not always produce peaceful feelings. Sometimes it can be very painful. A Christian sister once came to Catherine when she was in the depths of despair and said,

> I've been tempted to feel sorry for you. Well, I'll be damned if I'll feel sorry for you. Forgive the language, but I feel just that vehemently about it. Pity wouldn't help you a bit. Besides, why should I pity you? You have all you need—the strength and guidance of God himself.[5]

Out of all the sympathy visits she had in those days after Peter's death, this one stuck out in Catherine's mind. It motivated her to withdraw from pitiful seclusion, which was doing her more harm than good. Most importantly, this incident taught her that sometimes God's comfort comes in the form of a gentle rebuke.

During those difficult days, as Catherine daily soaked her mind in God's Word, she came to discover that "Scripture bathes the subject of death and immortality in the sunlight of normalcy, lifts it out of the realm of the dark and sinister unknown."[6] This was the next phase in her journey through grief. She found

---

[4]*Meeting God at Every Turn*, 108.
[5]Ibid., 110.
[6]Ibid., 111.

blessed assurance in the reality of the afterlife.

So the Lord carried Catherine through these divine truths and, through the arms of sympathetic friends, wrapped His love around her. But He did not shield her from the "what if" stage. She walked through this phase with the help of her mother and Rebecca Beard, a close friend. In their presence, she unleashed all of her anger and frustration, first on herself and then on God.

Neither her mother nor her friend offered Catherine any words. They simply listened to her with open, nonjudgmental hearts. Then they held her and prayed with her. It was at this point that the healing process began. As Catherine put it:

> "In God's own time," [Mother] told me quietly, "you will get God's answers." Mother knew so well that God alone can finally heal the brokenhearted. Grief is a mutilation, a gaping hole in the human spirit. . . . Some beloved person has been wrested, torn bodily from one's life. The hurt is nonetheless factual even though the family physician cannot clinically prove it. . . .
>
> It was Rebecca Beard, a human doctor, who helped to put my sore heart into the hands of the Great Physician. . . . Her prayer was a simple, heartfelt claiming of Christ's promise to bind up the brokenhearted. My heart had been broken and emptied. Now was the time to ask that He take it, make it whole again, and fill it up with His love. . . . And I knew that from that moment the healing had begun somewhere in the depths of my being.[7]

Part of her healing process included the emergence

---

[7]Ibid., 114–115.

of her childhood dream to become a writer. As she said in her journal,

> I must use part of my Quiet Time, to hear what the Lord has for me to do. He has indicated that He does have a plan for my life. Could it be that my dream of being a writer is part of this plan? I must be open to everything that could lead to this: letters, invitations, counsel of friends.

After this, the Lord made it abundantly clear to Catherine that writing was indeed a part of His plan for her life. The letters, invitations, and counsel from friends came in abundance. They all urged her to publish some of her husband's sermons. As it turned out, she had six hundred manuscripts from Peter's own hand.

At this time in her life, Catherine knew no one in the publishing business. So she prayed for the Lord to open a contact if this was His will. Not long after this, three publishing houses sent her letters asking her if she would be willing to compile and edit some of Peter's prayers and sermons.

Catherine chose to work with the Fleming H. Revell Company, which offered her a contract to publish a minimum of twelve of Peter's sermons. Much to everyone's surprise, except for Catherine's, the compilation, which was entitled *Mr. Jones, Meet the Master*, became a huge bestseller.

The success of the book led Edward Aswell at the McGraw-Hill Company to offer Catherine a contract to edit another book of Peter's sermons. She countered with a suggestion that she write about the man behind the sermons. Not convinced of her writing ability, Mr. Aswell cautiously agreed to look at a couple of her sample chapters.

For days Catherine struggled with developing an outline and producing sample chapters. Then, in an inspired moment in the middle of the night, she wrote a piece about the last words Peter had spoken to her. She also wrote a humorous piece about some of Peter's playful antics.

After reading her material, Mr. Aswell immediately offered her a contract to write *A Man Called Peter*, which was published in 1951. The book was on the *New York Times* bestseller list for more than fifty consecutive weeks. Then, in 1955, *A Man Called Peter* was made into a successful movie.

In the midst of her grieving process, the Lord opened the floodgates of heaven and blessed her abundantly. As a result, the fears about her financial situation quickly subsided. She did not have to sell her car or the Cape Cod cottage.

After two years in a small apartment in Washington, she was able to buy a home in a nearby neighborhood. God had graciously taken care of Catherine's and Peter John's economic needs solely through her book royalties.

Despite her joy over her book success, a conflict began to swirl around in Catherine's soul concerning the role of women in the world. She had been raised to believe that the woman's place was in the home. And she was married to a man who had strong convictions about this, as well. Quite frankly, Catherine had always associated true femininity with the home.

But widowhood had forced her into the workaday world. And she was not sure it was possible to be feminine in this new environment. The aggressiveness and independence needed in the business world seemed to be in direct contradiction to her femininity. Mrs. Marshall described her dilemma in this way:

Looking back now, I know that this was only the beginning of a conflict that was to go on for a long time and become even more poignant before it could be resolved. There was no clash between my ideal of a woman's role in the world and the writing itself. Always the pencil in my hand meant joy. My difficulty was that of reconciling myself to the commercial aspects of the book world, to my writing being in any way connected with earning a living. The conflict in me was therefore basically a clash between femininity and the career that pressed in upon me. The woman and the book were in headlong collision.[8]

While all these thoughts and emotions were tumbling around in Catherine's mind, another storm was brewing. While she was well into her journey through grief to healing, Peter John was just beginning to ask questions.

At nine years of age, he had not fully comprehended what it meant for him to lose his father. He had given himself over to silence and avoided any discussion about his father's death. Catherine tried to draw him out but often failed to get more than one or two words out of him at a time.

To break through his wall of defense, Catherine attempted to get involved in his world. Though she loathed them, she went to baseball and football games with Peter. Catherine's father also spent many hours with him, and so did some of the men from church. But none of this seemed to help break down his emotional barriers. She consulted counselor after counselor, but still there was no breakthrough.

These barriers frustrated Catherine. But some of

---

[8]*To Live Again*, 102.

his teenage behaviors really hurt her. At fourteen years of age, she caught him smoking. Another time he confessed to having read "sex-saturated novels." On another occasion he and some buddies got into trouble with the law for destroying school property.

Faced with such trials, as always, Catherine turned to the Lord. Her best guidance came through her daily devotional time with Him. She was thankful that she had trained her heart to know His voice while she was in the "school of green pastures." And the Lord rewarded her consistent obedience by telling her specific ways in which to help her son.

The instructions she received were practical, and the insights could be helpful for any parent. The Lord gave her the following detailed directions:

> [You are] to make a date with Peter John to go over finances. Through this he will begin to feel needed. [You are] to praise him more. Try the power of praise for him a lot more often. Question: What is he to do on Friday and Saturday nights? There has to be real planning ahead on this. . . .
>
> Do not be afraid for young Peter. No harm will come to him. He also is My child. I love him more than you do! . . .
>
> You have still not completely released Peter to Me. Don't strain too much after it though. It will come gradually, if you let Me do it—even as a plant grows under My care, so a child grows. . . .
>
> You are fearful for Peter because of deep-hidden guilt concerning him. Fear usually comes from guilt. You feel instinctively—and rightly so—that where you fail to supply strong enough discipline, then I, Peter's heavenly Father, will have to permit those disciplines to be supplied by hard and difficult circumstances. Not enough parents face up to this.

You must quietly get My mind and direction about Peter in these areas and then act upon My guidance. As you do act, your fear will leave. But let Me warn you about this. Don't let your time with Me or what I am telling you lull you into a sense of false security or be a substitute for action—or the fear will return in full force.

Here are my instructions:

1. TV and movies: You are to keep a careful check on what he sees. Plan ahead. Be so well informed about films and TV programs that you will earn Peter's respect in this regard. When there is no good movie on a Saturday, some other activity must be planned ahead. Often you have taken the line of least resistance because you haven't been prepared with adequate information.

2. Tidiness and taking care of his own clothes: Insist that he take responsibility here.

3. Money, allowance, etc.: You have not been handling this properly. You must take time—over and over—to come back to Me to think these matters through.

Through Catherine's obedience to the Lord's practical counsel, things began to improve between herself and her son. But the Lord showed her further that she needed to be completely open with Peter and honest with him about her own spiritual and emotional struggles. As she did this, the pretenses between the two of them slowly began to drop, and their relationship took a turn in the right direction.

Not long after this, Catherine was driving Peter to college. Several years earlier she had said good-bye to her beloved husband. Now she was bidding at least a temporary farewell to her son. Another era was quickly coming to a close for her. With its passing, feelings of loneliness slowly began to creep in. "I must realize," she confessed in her journal, "that loneliness, that sense of dissatisfaction, that feeling of some happiness just eluding me, is in all human beings, and is put there by God to keep us searching after Him. Perhaps when I just 'settle down' to this doubtful state of single blessedness, inner peace will come. We shall see."

But Catherine's inner churning continued. Several years after Peter's death, she was still giving in to the whims of self-pity. When she would see couples walking down the street, she would inwardly seethe with jealously. When she attended church or political socials and found that she was the only single person there, she would ask, "Why me?"

What caused most of the tension in Catherine's soul was her conviction that remarriage would betray the precious memory of Peter. She could not bring herself to be untrue in any way to the man she so loved.

In time, however, her feelings slowly began to change on this matter. She thought that the Lord might be opening the door for her to pursue a new relationship. So when men began to call her for dates, she accepted.

Catherine soon found herself particularly interested in Howard, a wealthy and handsome businessman from South Carolina. They met while she was speaking at a Washington dinner party, and almost immediately there was an attraction between the two of them.

Howard was a widower with two teenage sons. Besides having some similar interests, the fact that they had both lost their spouses gave them a lot of common ground. Before long, Catherine was convinced that Howard was the one for her. Her journal entries at this point reveal her growing confidence:

> The revelation today is that there has to be someone else for me into whose life I can pour everything. Since this is what my whole being cries out for, it is as sure of fulfillment as that the tides of the ocean will come in again. Somewhere there is a man whose life needs this lavish giving, whose personality and career will bloom and blossom under it. Whether that man be Howard, only God knows at this point—though my heart says "yes. . . ."

> Today God gave me a beautiful gift, mainly, the assurance that remarriage is His idea not mine. He wants it for me even more than I want it. But a gift is not truly ours until we take it.

> So I accept it with gratitude. This means that I no longer have to worry about whether it's right to marry again; all I do have to do is to give thanks to God that the matter is settled and relax until God's time comes to meet "the man."

> I see that only now—after almost seven years—am I finally ready really to accept Peter's death fully, really ready to shut the door on the past and go out into a new life. Obviously, remarriage couldn't happen until this step was taken on my part. No man wants to be part of my old life. It's incredible perhaps that it has taken me so long to come to this position.

But Howard was not to be the one for her. Catherine soon realized this and was heartbroken over the situation. First, Howard showed very little interest in Christianity. Second, his work schedule and travel kept them separated for long periods of time. After several long months of silence, Catherine received a note from him saying that he was about to be married to someone else.

Catherine recovered, and other dates followed. Jim, an acquaintance from church, was the next man to play an important role in her life. Their relationship started with Catherine's concern for Peter John. She felt that he needed a father figure in his life, and she simply could not fill that role.

So the pastor of her church introduced Jim to Peter, and the two of them started hunting together. Jim lived in Wyoming but frequently came to Washington on business. Whenever he was in town, he made a point to get together with the boy. Catherine was thankful that Jim was willing to fill this void in her son's life.

After a couple of months, Jim started to come by the house to visit Peter John. Over coffee, he would discuss his marital problems with Catherine. Warning signs quickly went up in Catherine's mind. Nevertheless, she thought she might be able to help him work out the differences with his wife.

One evening, Jim confessed to Catherine that he had fallen in love with her and that he intended to get a divorce. A flurry of emotions converged in Catherine's heart. She liked Jim very much, but she also knew that God could never honor this kind of relationship.

Though she knew it would devastate him, Catherine wrote Jim a letter ending anything between them. This was not easy to do because it would mean for her another loss. But she also knew all along that her motives had not been right in the relationship. She was simply trying to alleviate her loneliness. As soon as she confessed her sin and let go, Catherine was able to see clearly what loneliness had driven her to do. The following are her insights as she recorded them in her journal:

For this past year, I have felt defeated and frustrated. And this certainly is not as God wishes it. Here are some of the ways I have allowed my loneliness to defeat me:

1. The salt, the savor has gone out of my life. Nothing, not even the very great success of *A Man Called Peter*, thrills me much now. "Success" has turned to ashes in my mouth. The zest has gone out of everyday life. This is wrong. It is the outlook of a dying creature—certainly not a "new creature in Christ Jesus."

2. There has been—over the past several years—a growing coldness in my heart toward other people rather than an increasing love and warmth. Visiting the sick has been a chore—no joy in it.

3. Along with the above, there has inevitably come an increasing preoccupation with self. Or perhaps the preoccupation with self is the real cause of the defeats.

4. I have sought satisfaction in material things and have not found anything here that lasts.

5. I have become more irritable in the daily grind of everyday life. Slow drivers, inept sales-girls, parking lot attendants, provoke me much more easily than they used to.

6. I have known that God wanted me to get up an hour earlier each morning for prayer and Bible reading, yet have not been consistent about this.

7. I have failed almost totally in small disci-plines of appetite—small self-denials which, at the time, I knew were right.

8. I have often failed to have the inner strength

to discipline or to say no to Peter John, when I
knew I should have.

9. Along with all these failures, I have often
had a feeling of superiority to other human beings—which makes no sense at all.

In plain and simple terms, Catherine's spiritual
life was all out of whack. She had been asking God to
approve *her* plans instead of waiting on Him each day
to reveal His will. She had come to the conclusion that
her self-will was at the root of all her problems.

Several years earlier, while she was leaving Peter's
deathbed, an invisible hand had tapped Catherine on
the shoulder. The voice of her Lord told her, *"Surely
goodness and mercy shall follow you all the days of
your life."* To this point in Catherine's life, the Lord's
goodness and mercy had been evident in every aspect.

But Catherine now came to learn that the Lord's
goodness and mercy sometimes comes at a cost. This
is because He requires the purification of those who
follow Him. The trials of grief and loneliness were His
tools for cleansing her. And she was to accept them as
coming from His hands.

She saw further that her stubborn willfulness was
thwarting God's purposes for her. So she resolutely
put the idea of remarriage directly in the Lord's
hands. She wrote in her journal:

I am to "seek the kingdom of God first" in regard to remarriage. Should this be God's will for
me, then in any given man I am to seek *first* those
inner qualities of mind and heart that belong to
God's kingdom. But what about *me*? What inner
qualities should I have to qualify to be a wife
again?

5

This Is Fun, But . . .

Lord, would You guide me to the woman You have selected to share my life?" Leonard LeSourd prayed one dark and dreary night. He uttered this urgent prayer while in the grip of discouragement. A single father of three young children—Linda, ten; Chester, six; and Jeffrey, three—he was desperate to find someone to help him carry the load.

Leonard's ten-year marriage to his children's mother, Eve, had crumbled shortly after she was committed to a state institution with severe alcohol problems. Len knew of her struggles before they married but believed that their love for Jesus and for each other would pull them through.

In the beginning, love seemed to be enough. This cord of three strands kept the two of them close and Eve's problems at bay. But when they moved from New York City to a countryside seventy-five miles away, Eve's emotional difficulties resurfaced.

The unfamiliar surroundings brought her turmoil to a head and drove her and the family to the brink of collapse. When counseling and therapy did not help her situation, she was hospitalized for seven months.

When that didn't work either, she was finally put in a mental institution by her physician-father.

All of these events had a devastating effect on Len and the children. Len went through a period of time when he doubted God's goodness. So he turned his back on the Lord and went his own way. Several months later, he came back to his senses, repented, and asked the Lord to forgive him.

In the process of time, Len also asked the Lord for a new life partner. He described what happened in this way:

> For me, it was a complete and senseless tragedy. In helpless frustration over a five-year period, I watched the life of the woman I loved deteriorate. Never had I even imagined such pain, such grief. It precipitated a crisis of faith. "Why, Lord, would You let this happen to me? I've tried to be a good husband, a good Christian. . . .
>
> God was silent. I've learned since that He has a way of giving those who belong to Him a long leash. So I turned my back on Him, tried to rediscover life in the fast lane. It didn't take much time for me to fall on my face. The attempt to resume my old lifestyle was a disaster for me and bad for the children.
>
> When I came back to Him on my knees, repentant, He was merciful. That was when, in response to my prayer for a new life partner, the name *Catherine Marshall* popped into my mind.[1]

Catherine and Len had met several years before when he had asked her to write an article for *Guideposts*, the magazine for which Len was the chief editor. But he did not know her at all in a personal way. Nev-

---

[1] *Light in My Darkest Night*, 26–27.

ertheless, in obedience to what he thought the Lord was telling him, Len contacted Catherine in Washington.

Subsequently, he flew to Washington where they met on a luncheon date to discuss some ideas for a future article. After two hours, they decided that she would write about the Holy Spirit, a subject of much interest to her since her illness several years before.

This was a professional meeting only. It seemed that Len was trying to decide whether this was really the Lord's will. Several months later, Len was convinced that the Lord was leading him to pursue Catherine. So in the summer of 1959, he sent Catherine a letter.

"I would like to know you better," he wrote. "How do you react to this idea? We'll choose a day, and then you write on your calendar three letters: FUN. I'll pick you up in the morning in my car, and we'll just take off to the beach or the mountains or whatever." They set a date early in August and ended that day having spent eleven hours together in nonstop conversation.

As it turned out, Len and Catherine had much in common. They were both preacher's children, both had close relations with their family, both were single parents, and both had a love of words. There was also an obvious physical attraction between the two of them.

However, while Catherine liked his approach to her, she was still reluctant, at first, to make a serious commitment to Len. The reason for this was his three small children. Peter John was already "out of the nest," and she was not prepared at age forty-five to take on a motherly responsibility again. Besides, Len was a divorced man, and she knew God hated divorce.

Len, on the other hand, knew that the divine hand

had brought them together. Within a very short period of time, he proposed to Catherine. Surprised and shocked by his quick proposal, she told him that she needed more time. Similar to the situation with Peter when he proposed to her, Catherine hesitated in order to seek God's guidance.

In her journal, Catherine described in detail her thoughts about remarriage and how the Lord revealed His will to her:

In my morning times, that still, small Voice in my inner spirit asked me some searching questions:

"Have you counted the cost? Have you really looked at the readjustments necessary for another marriage? Are there not certain areas of your life where rigidity is creeping in? The rough and tumble of family life is My antidote to rigidity. But are you willing to be cured? And do you not realize that My way would be to send you a man not just to satisfy your own needs, but because he has gigantic needs himself?"

The issue was whether I was ready for that much commitment, not just to a man, but to three children, too. Part of me was excited and stirred; the other part wanted to flee. Both Len and I were agreed on the need to put Jesus at the center of any remarriage. Still I hung back. . . .

I thought with longing of the new house being built for me in Washington. It was almost finished. Adjoining my bedroom, cut off from the rest of the house, would be a step-down room where I could write. It would be my sanctuary. I was most reluctant to give up that prospect. . . .

Two roads stretched ahead, and I was at the parting of the ways. In that house being built I might produce many articles and books. There I would have a cushioned, sheltered life—yes, and probably a lonely one. And, if I chose the other road, I would plunge directly back into turbulent life. . . . "Lord," I prayed one September morning in 1959, "I don't understand at all. Are You in this?"

I took a deep breath, for there was a sudden luminosity about this moment that I recognized. It had happened before when I asked Him for understanding. Once again, no illumination came to my mind. Instead, there was the overwhelming sense of His presence. . . .

Suddenly, the choice God was presenting to me was clear. To say yes to this man I loved, taking his children into my heart and life, meant a difficult adjustment. Yet I saw that if I said no and chose the other road, I would be turning away from the mainstream of life. The "no" way would be comfortable, but it would take me farther and farther from contact with people—and, ultimately, from God who shapes us through the people He places in our path. At that moment His command seemed clear—"Say yes to life."[2]

On November 14, 1959, after only a few months of courtship, Len and Catherine were married. They moved to Chappaqua, a countryside town in Westchester County about forty-five miles from New York City. Catherine had an office at home, while Len continued to work as executive editor for *Guideposts*.

Each morning Len and Catherine arose early to read the Word and pray together. They shared many exciting spiritual and emotional discoveries. Among the most important things they learned right at the start of their relationship was that God keeps the fun

---

[2]Ibid., 22–23.

in love and romance. He keeps the flame of love alive between two people who are open to Him.

Indeed, their relationship was characterized by fun, even as it was on their first date. But, throughout their years together, there was one thing that kept resurfacing and putting a damper on their gaiety: the divorce issue. Catherine was haunted by the fact of Len's divorce.

She did not discuss the issue in her books out of respect for Len and for fear that her readership might think she approved of such a practice. But her journals, which were not published at the time, are chockfull of her thoughts and struggles about it. In 1989, six years after her death, Len published these journals.

He did this because he thought it might benefit her readers in two ways. First, it would show vividly the pain and grief associated with divorce and its repercussions on the entire family. Second, it would reveal how they together worked through the difficult issues surrounding divorce and remarriage.

Through the intimate details shared in her journals, both Len and Catherine let their readers enter into their most private world. While Catherine eventually came to peace about her situation, she did not know what her experience could mean for others.

Len thought that, as with every other aspect of Catherine's life, her readers could gain comfort and insight from how she honestly dealt with her shortcomings in this situation and from how she earnestly sought the Lord in her time of trouble. The following is a selection from a series of conversations between Len and Catherine and a few excerpts from her journal entries:

(Before their marriage)

Len: Catherine and I discussed the situation in depth, talked with Christian counselors and pastors ... receiving a bewildering variety of opinions. Catherine agonized over this, praying about it for weeks.

Finally she shared with me the word she believed she had received: *The Lord is in the business of restoring broken homes and healing damaged families. He hates divorce, as He hates all sin, for the harm it does in every life it touches. But He does not lock us into our sins; He is the God of redemption and new beginnings. . . .*

(Eight years into the marriage, spring 1967)

Catherine: Lord, I come to You each morning for a time of fellowship together ... to share my concerns, to feel Your love, to receive Your guidance and, yes, even Your reproof.

Len and I had a heated session the other night during which he spoke words of correction to me about my tendency to be critical, my aloofness from people, my inability to demonstrate love even to certain members of my own family. I knew there was truth in what he said, and he did it lovingly, but I was resistant. . . .

Jesus, I hear You speak even as I write these words on paper. Len, as my husband, is the spiritual head of our home. He has the right, even the responsibility, to correct the members of his family. I need to see You in Len and trust that You are working in him.

But I confess something else here, Lord. I continue to be troubled in my spirit about Len's divorce. I thought I heard Your will on this before I married him. . . . Perhaps the real reason for my uneasiness is the question I keep asking myself: "Did I have the right to remarry? Was that in any way a betrayal of Peter?"

Perhaps I only kidded and rationalized myself into thinking that I did have Your approval to remarry. Could the truth have been for me that I was meant to be content in the state in which I found myself after Peter's death? After You Yourself had opened the door into the writing world for me, and authored my books and blessed them immeasurably, did You not mean for me to be grateful and to leave it there?

In marrying Len, was I not manipulating? Was it man-made, not God-given? Was it the result of my rebelling against the single condition to which You had called me, thereby violating a law of the Spirit? So now—I open myself to Your mercy, Lord. You alone can help me through this situation. . . .

(A conversation between Catherine and Len, spring 1971; Len is narrating)

Catherine: "I wasn't really prepared to take on three small children when I married you."

We were back on rocky terrain. Familiar ground, especially in recent years. "Why do you keep bringing this up?"

"Because it's constantly on my mind. I feel that I'm living outside of God's will."

"You certainly didn't feel that way the first ten years of our marriage."

"At times I did. The pace of our lives back then was so fast I just didn't dwell on it."

"What you're saying, Catherine, is that when things were going well for you, you felt you were in God's will. Now that your book *Gloria* is not going well, and you have some relationship problems inside and outside the family, then you're out of God's will. And so you place the blame on the fact that you married a divorced man."

"It goes much deeper than that," Catherine replied. "I thought I'd heard God on the matter of your divorce before you and I were married. The unrest in my spirit began about five years ago. It came from—well, I'm not sure just where."

I struggled with a growing irritation that I knew I had to keep under control. . . . "What does this add up to now—today? Certainly not another divorce. Separation? How would that go down with your readers? We're really between a rock and a hard place, aren't we?"

Catherine nodded. "What you're saying is that I have to work this out between God and me."

"What I'm saying is, look at the positive accomplishments you and I have achieved together over the past twelve years. Shall I list them?"

"That's not necessary. I agree there are many."

"Then why would God bless our marriage so much if we are out of His will?"

Catherine shook her head. "I'm sure lots of people who are way out of God's will are accomplishing things that appear to be blessed. That has nothing to do with the feeling of unrest I have about our marriage. It's troubled me for years. . . . The question I have for you, Len, is: What about your attitudes? What do you need to change?

"About our marriage?"

"Well, yes. But I was thinking more about your divorce."

"I don't understand. A divorce is a divorce. What can you change about that?"

"You can't change the fact of a divorce, but you can change your attitude about it."

Taken by surprise, I struggled to put my thoughts together. "Divorce is always a tragedy. It's a terrible failure. But for some marriages, it seems to be the only answer. I tried for years to save my first marriage. Nothing seemed to help. The divorce and remarriage gave my children a chance for a stable home, a normal childhood. For me . . . well, it freed me to find the creative life God had for me."

"Len, you're not really sure of that. God's perfect plan for you might have been to stick with the marriage, in spite of Eve's alcoholism, to work out a productive balance that could have had positive results beyond your wildest dreams."

I stared at Catherine in amazement . . . speechless for a long stretch as I got very busy sorting some papers. Deep down I had to admit Catherine had scored a point. And I realized something else. Though unsettling, there was also something deeply fulfilling in these confrontations with Catherine. How I loved to watch her mental processes in action. How I loved her. Period. . . .

(A conversation between Len and Catherine, fall 1971; Len is narrating)

"I hope you never change, Catherine. Your quest for excellence shines through all your books. You get the absolute maximum from your talent. But how much can you—should you—transfer this to those close to you? . . . It used to bother me a lot. I didn't feel enough of your love went along with this toughness. I'm beginning to change my mind about this, however, and you need to know this."

"In what way, Len?"

"The past months have been a real learning time for me, too. In looking back at my first marriage, I see how I tried to smooth over the difficulties, rationalizing that I was a peacemaker.

When his home situation is in chaos, a man tends to seek peace at any price. When you and the others pointed this out to me on Cape Cod last summer, I resisted it. But it's true. In my first marriage I now think I did damage to Eve by not confronting her more. I covered up for her too much, ducked the truth. . . . I thank God now for the way you came into our family of four confused, bruised individuals and set tough, high standards for every one of us. . . ."

"I think I know what else you're thinking," Catherine said softly. "It concerns our marriage."

"Your perfectionism has made it difficult at times. My divorce, for example, is the essence of imperfection."

"That's true, Len. I wanted to ignore it, pretend it never happened. That was foolish of me. I let it fester inside."

"But God heals these wounds. He restores. He reconciles."

"I know that, and I'm struggling with all that right now. Forgive me for being the way I am. I can't seem to help it. I need to hear from the Lord. He is guiding me in so many ways now. I'm sure He'll give me His word about this, too."[3]

It is evident through these conversations between Len and Catherine and her many journal entries that a critical spirit and a perfectionist attitude were the culprits behind much of her anxiety over his divorce. But the beauty of this entire process was Catherine's honesty and frankness, both before her God and Len.

For the twenty-three years of their marriage, Len and Catherine together consistently rose early in the morning to meet with their God before they started

---

[3]Ibid., 27, 52–53, 74–77, 216–217.

their day. This gave them the strength and wisdom not only to tackle Catherine's issues concerning their marriage, but also to embrace the challenges of daily life with three small children.

In the first few years in her new role as wife and mother, these quiet times with her husband were Catherine's only taste of tranquillity. She did not realize it in the beginning, but they would be the only means by which God would prepare her for the unexpected twists and turns of blended family life.

6

The School of Family Life

It had been one of those mornings. First, there was loud screaming coming from the boys' room. Jeff had just bit Chester; but, according to Jeff, Chester had kicked him first. Then Linda came out of her room barefooted on the cold wooden floor. When Catherine told her to put her slippers on, Linda claimed she could not get them on because the washing machine had shrunk them.

Breakfast had yet to be started, lunches were not yet made, and the school bus was about to pull up any minute. In the middle of food preparation, the doorbell rang, then the telephone rang. Then Chester spilled jam on his pants and had to change them. Peter John yelled from the other room that he could not find any underwear.

When she finally got everyone out of the house, Catherine sunk into her easy chair with a cup of coffee in her hand. "Lord," she prayed, "what is this about anyway? When You put people together in families, just what did You really have in mind? . . . Are you sure this family bit is not one of Your sneaky tricks?"[1]

---

[1]*Meeting God at Every Turn*, 198.

In the process of the daily grind, the Lord showed Catherine that the family was God's training ground for life. Where else, she reasoned, could we learn about such virtues as patience and forgiveness? Catherine also saw vividly how God molds character and chisels out the personality in the context of family life. She had this to say about His practical approach:

> I was also learning that most of us are not anything like as realistic as our God. We like to deal with high-flown theological abstractions. (After all, they can be kept at safe arm's length.) He deals with the lilies of the field, the yeast in the housewife's bread, patches on garments, and curing Grandmother's arthritis. So of course the master design for us to advance toward our heavenly home via the nitty-gritty of family life would be just like Him.[2]

Those early morning devotions yielded for Catherine much insight into this idea of the family as a conduit for learning God's truths. One of her journal entries says this:

> Our very first step in solving family problems is resolutely to view our particular difficulties as God's schoolroom for the truths He longs to teach us and the immense riches of His glory He wants to pour into our lives—if only we will let Him. He's going to have to be our Teacher all the way. What's required of us is the open-mindedness of the eager learner, plus taking the time day by day to submit practical questions to Him.[3]

Morning by morning, Len and Catherine hurled

---

[2]Ibid., 198.
[3]Ibid., 196.

practical prayers toward heaven. Len started to keep a prayer notebook in which he recorded their prayers and God's answers. Some of their most repeated requests were as follows:

1. That household help be found so that Catherine can continue the writing of her novel *Christy*.
2. That Peter will forget trying to be a playboy at Yale and find God's purpose for his life.
3. That Linda will stop rebelling against authority at home and at school.
4. That Chester will learn to control his temper and accept his new home situation.
5. That we can find the way to get Jeff out of diapers at night.[4]

Answers came but not always the ways they expected them. A reliable housekeeper was eventually found so that Catherine could devote her mornings to writing. A country practitioner advised Catherine to take the diapers off Jeff at night. Once he got a taste of sleeping in a wet bed, he would be motivated to get up and go to the bathroom. She did it, and, within a few weeks, he was out of diapers.

The Lord also gave Catherine some practical household rules:

1. Meals at regular hours and at least the evening meal eaten together as a family unit whenever possible. Dinner thus to be the focal point of each day. . . .
2. Regular bedtime, though later on the weekends.
3. No television for children on school nights.

---

[4]Ibid., 200.

TV and movies on weekends to be screened carefully.

4. Linda's endless telephone conversations with friends to be limited to one period, 3:30–6:00 each afternoon. No twosome dates until she is sixteen.

5. Time to be given to children on weekends for family outings and/or home games.

6. On Sundays go as a family to church.

7. Len and I to share checking on children's school homework. Our full interest and participation in the PTA and all school events pertaining to our three.

8. Discipline always to be a part of our life together; punishment to fit the disobedience; spankings by no means ruled out.[5]

While they were not always easily implemented, these household rules made a difference in the LeSourd home. The atmosphere was calmer, and chaos was kept at a minimum. Yet the most important lesson Catherine learned from this is that things always went smoother when, rather than going her own way in her own wisdom, she waited on the Lord.

But waiting was not always easy. Much to Catherine's frustration at times, prayers concerning her two teenagers, Linda and Peter, seemed to bounce off the ceiling. To Catherine, there seemed to be no change in the reckless courses of their lives. The tension mounted, especially between her and Linda, as she tried to help them to see the error of their ways.

In 1963, after a trip to the Holy Land, Catherine came down with a severe case of bronchitis. When it threatened to turn into a chronic lung ailment, the

[5]Ibid., 202–203.

doctor urged her to move to a warmer climate. In 1964, the LeSourds bought a home in Boynton Beach, Florida. Len commuted back and forth between Florida and his job in New York City.

This juggling of life between two states only added to the emotional strain already plaguing the family. As their communication suffered, Catherine and Len became distant from each other, both spiritually and emotionally. The boys had adjusted well to the move and to the new school. But Linda was a different story. She became more and more unmanageable, and Catherine was at a loss to know how to handle her.

From the very beginning there was tension between the two of them. Catherine described her disillusionment in this way:

> There were occasions when I felt close to this gifted but often troubled girl, more times when I felt like a rejected parent. I struggled with all of the negative stepmother images. Often I caught myself resenting this child and her attitudes. Since this was not my image of the "good mother," I tried to ignore or bury such emotions. . . .
>
> I would seek God's help for this in my Quiet Times. He met me one Sunday in church. The winter sunlight was streaming in the tall arched windows laying long patterns of light across the white colonial sanctuary. I was sitting there thinking about Linda. Suddenly in my mind and heart His voice was speaking to me with particular clarity and intensity. *Unless you love her, you don't love Me.*
>
> *Lord, I know that's true.* The thought stabbed me. *But how do we love certain persons when we hate some of the things they do? Please tell me how. And, Lord, I have another problem. I can't manu-*

*facture love. Nobody can. How can I manage it un-
less You give me that love as a sheer gift?*[6]

Linda, too, described some of her battles with life
and with her stepmother:

> So many emotions were churning around in-
> side me when Dad remarried. At ten I thought I
> was pretty adult. But looking back, I realize I was
> in great need of someone who understood my con-
> fused thoughts and emotions and could have
> helped me sort them out. . . .
>
> When Dad married Catherine (Mom, as I soon
> called her), I was excited. It signaled a return to
> normalcy. And a bestselling author seemed so
> glamorous to me! I'd even have an older brother,
> her son Peter, a tall, handsome, worldly-wise col-
> lege sophomore. . . .
>
> When Dad returned from his honeymoon with
> our new "Mom," they moved into a new house in
> a new community. Soon my brothers and I joined
> them—and right away I could see that things
> were not going to be as great as I had thought. As
> the new girl in my fifth-grade class, I guess I tried
> too hard to show my classmates how great our
> family was: my dad an important editor . . . my
> new mother a famous writer . . . my big brother at
> Yale. It was too heady for a ten-year-old to handle
> very well.
>
> My stepmother and I soon began to clash over
> all sorts of things: clothes, food, bedtime, money,
> duties around the house. For someone who had
> had very little discipline up to then, this super-
> structured new home life came as a blow. To make
> things worse, I felt I had lost my father. When he

---

[6]Ibid., 207–208.

wasn't working in Manhattan, he and Mom were going places, doing things, often without me and the boys. It seemed that we saw more of the live-in housekeeper than our parents.

Eventually I made it into the "in" crowd at school. That entailed "hanging out" at local restaurants, weekend parties, trying out alcohol and cigarettes. All of these things were forbidden to me, and I chafed at being the most restricted of the group. Occasionally I would sneak out of the house to join my friends, or lock myself into the bathroom to smoke. When Mom caught me at these things, there were some pretty bad scenes. Even Dad was upset with me at times, but usually he'd just leave the room, and later I could hear raised voices behind my parents' door.

My schoolwork was another battleground. Though I had always been a straight-A student, my grades now seesawed wildly. Sadly, I think it was my way of "getting back" at my parents; no doubt it was also a cry for help. . . .

Mom was warm and nice to me when I followed the rules at home and performed well in school. But I didn't feel she understood me—or wanted to try. I knew Dad loved me, but most of his time seemed to be spent smoothing over conflict between Mom and me. I'd been his "Number One girl" for so long—now I felt I'd lost him. As I entered my teens I was a very unhappy girl.[7]

Peter John was displaying some rebellion of his own. By the time he had graduated from Yale University, he had strayed far from the Lord. He did not care about where he was going or what he would do with his life. Catherine continued to pray for him often, but

[7]*Light in My Darkest Night*, 44–46.

the apathy persisted. Peter explained his state of mind with these words:

> If there was ever a lost soul, wandering about without purpose or direction, it was me in the summer of 1961. Having graduated from Yale University, I had come home to the red-shuttered house in Chappaqua with all my belongings—and no idea what to do next. I had no career plans (what does one do with a history degree if one doesn't want to teach?) and, to put it bluntly, no remote idea why I was living.
>
> Up to this point, my life had been one of almost total self-centeredness, for I had withdrawn after my father's death into a world of lonely independence from everybody, including God. During my college years at Old Eli I had tried to fill the emptiness with the proverbial "wine, women, and song"; now in Chappaqua, daily tennis matches were all that got me out of bed in the morning.[8]

Late in the summer of 1961, a miraculous change took place in Peter. He met Jesus at a conference of the Fellowship of Christian Athletes and, in one startling moment, surrendered his life to Him. All that his mother taught him about Christ came flooding back into his memory, and he could not resist the One who was calling him. What took place after this Peter could have never expected. In his own words:

> Toward the end of the conference, I waited until everyone else had left the large wooden auditorium, then went up to speak with Moomaw. I told him I had some questions about dating, but the Spirit of God enabled Donn to see through this

---

[8]Ibid., 36–37.

smokescreen. "That's not what's the matter with you," he said. "Your problem is that you've been running away from God all your life. When are you going to be ready to give your life to Jesus Christ?"

Suddenly I had the strange sensation of standing about twenty feet away from myself, hearing myself say something I had no intention of saying. To my astonishment, what came out of me was: "Well, I guess I'm ready as I'll ever be. . . ."

I knew what I was doing; my mother had always made it clear that giving your life to Christ meant giving up control, coming under His authority to live the rest of your life for His plans, not your own.

My prayer was short, even crude: "Lord, my life is a mess. I have fouled it all up, and I'm sick of running it my way. You can have the whole stinking pile of garbage, and if You can do anything with it, it's all Yours. . . ." Now that I was seeking His will for my life, God moved with a speed that took my breath away. . . .

In August I was accepted for the September entering class at Princeton Seminary. Amazing—in that only a few weeks before all this, becoming a Christian, let alone a Christian minister, was the farthest thing from my mind!

And so now after years of avoiding God, I was following in my father's footsteps. What Jesus will do with my life, how He will lead me, remains to be seen. But at last I know that I am finally tracking with His loving plan for my life.[9]

Ten years later, in the summer of 1971, that same divine Presence that took hold of Peter's life also en-

---

[9]Ibid., 37–38.

veloped Linda's life. She described that miraculous moment in this way:

> On the afternoon after my arrival at Cape Cod, I was about to take a shower. A particular moment is crystallized forever for me. I had one foot on the bathroom rug, the other in the shower stall. At that instant, like a bolt, the realization hit me that one foot in, one foot out was an accurate representation of my life so far. Several times I'd gone through the motions of committing my life to God. Yet I did not have an obedient heart. I was living in outright rebellion against Him.
>
> I sensed that this was the moment to decide— for Him or against Him. There could no longer be any middle ground.
>
> Standing there, I carefully weighed what choosing the Lord's side would cost me. Obviously, some things in my life would have to go. But I was tired of living in two worlds and not enjoying either. Desperately, I longed for His peace in my heart. I took a deep breath and said aloud, "I choose You, Lord." Then I got in the shower. That shower was my true baptism.[10]

Catherine's prayers were finally answered—in God's time, not hers. Peter and Linda joined their brothers, Chester and Jeff, in a life committed to Christ. When they were older, Chester and Jeff praised their stepmother for her tough stance with them and her prayer-centered life. Her devotion had set them on the right track for life.

Such were some of the trials and triumphs in Catherine's experience in the school of family life. The Lord taught her first and foremost that her commitment to

---

[10]*Meeting God at Every Turn*, 211–212.

Him did not guarantee that her children would always walk the straight and narrow path of salvation.

Nevertheless, her prayers made a difference, both in them and in her. As she entered into the prime of her life, Catherine thought, "Surely now in my latter years I'll be able to put to good use what wisdom I have accumulated." She believed, after all she had learned in the Lord's schoolrooms, she had now come to a place where she could guide her grown children in the faith.

Instead, Catherine soon found out that she still had a lot of growing up to do herself. The tools the Lord used to complete His unfinished work in her were again pain and grief unimaginable. Catherine thought she had learned all she needed to through trials and tribulations.

But their unexpected revisitation showed Catherine the hardness of heart that still plagued her. These excruciating experiences later in her life plunged her into a period of darkness greater than she had ever known.

7

Through the Valley of Death's Shadow

While at Princeton Seminary, Peter John met and married Edith Wallis, the daughter of medical missionaries to Guatemala. She was everything Catherine had hoped for in a daughter-in-law, the answer to her many prayers for her son. After graduation, Peter John and Edith moved to West Hartford, Connecticut, where he took a position as an assistant pastor.

On December 3, 1967, their first child, Peter Christopher, was born. Peter quickly called his mother in New York to give her the news that it was a boy and that something was terribly wrong with him. Poor muscle tone and lung congestion with a threat of pneumonia was the early diagnosis. Catherine wanted to come right away, but Peter urged her to wait until they knew more.

Early one morning, however, the Lord spoke to Catherine and told her that it was time to go see the child. He also gave her these instructions, *"Go—and crown my prince with thanksgiving."* While she was delayed at the airport, a sudden heaviness of spirit swept over Catherine. She was later to find out that it was right at that moment that the baby stopped breathing.

Thankfully, some friends of the Marshalls laid hands on the baby, and he revived. When Catherine arrived at the hospital, little Peter Christopher looked perfectly normal. But within a few hours after Catherine's arrival, the baby died. Catherine described what took place in those precious moments before and after his death:

> With Peter and Edith standing by the crib, and the doctor and nurses looking on from a discreet distance, I gently laid my hands on the soft skin of that little head. "You gave him, Lord. He is Your prince, You told me. We hereby, according to Your instruction, crown Peter Christopher with thanksgiving, the golden crown of gratitude for this life You have given."
>
> Thirty-five minutes later, the young doctor sadly informed us, "He is gone." It was almost as if that gentle spirit had been hanging on until I got there to bestow the blessing. All of us present tried to minister to Peter and Edith; I struggled with my own emotions. *Lord, I don't understand. When Peter Marshall died, Your sure word to me was that "goodness and mercy" would follow me all the days of my life. Lord, is this goodness and mercy?*
>
> I looked at Edith, her face wet with tears. Edith, born to be a mother. *What about it, Lord? Is Edith, then, not to know the joy of motherhood? And am I, then, not to be a grandmother?*[1]

---

[1]*Meeting God at Every Turn*, 222.

Two and a half years later, Catherine's searching questions were positively answered. Edith gave birth to Mary Elizabeth Marshall, a healthy baby girl. Catherine, who soon fell in love with being a grandmother, spent every free moment she could with Mary Elizabeth. The child filled Catherine's life with new adventures and joy unspeakable.

After a short stay in Connecticut, Peter was called to the pastorate at the First Wesleyan Community Church in East Dennis, Massachusetts. Then on July 22, 1971, Edith gave birth to her third child, Amy Catherine Marshall. But the joy that filled the hospital room at Mary Elizabeth's birth was not to be for this child.

The same problems that took the life of Peter Christopher were apparent in Amy Catherine. The disorder was identified by doctors as "genetic aberration cerebro-hepato-renal syndrome," a disease that affects the healthy development of the brain, liver, and kidneys. Both Peter and Edith carried the recessive gene, which meant that one out of four of their offspring could be affected.

From a medical standpoint, there was no hope for children born with this syndrome. Life expectancy was about six months at best. Catherine was not ready to give up so easily. She had lost one grandchild to this disease; she was not about to lose another.

With the aggressiveness so fitting her character, Catherine set out to storm the gates of heaven for her granddaughter. First, the family, along with a few close neighbors, gathered together for a time of intense prayer at Peter and Edith's home in East Dennis.

Pat, a friend who was known for her experience as an intercessor, received a word from the Lord for the family. They were to overcome their discouragement over the medical diagnosis, and they were not to deny Amy Catherine any ministry. Catherine was greatly encouraged by this message and took it as a call to battle.

Indeed, there was at least one encouraging sign. The next day Catherine and Peter drove to Boston to see the baby. It had been thirty-six hours since her birth, and she still had not wet her diapers, a sure indication that her kidneys were not functioning. Nevertheless, Catherine boldly told the nurse that they had come to pray for her healing. The nurse looked at her incredulously and told her the grim prognosis: "The baby has many problems. There have been multiple seizures. Please don't get your hopes up."

Peter then explained to the nurse that he believed God would heal her. He anointed Amy Catherine with oil and placed her in her grandmother's arms. Shortly after this, a prayer warrior from Peter's church had a vision that the baby's kidneys would function. In a matter of moments, they started working! Catherine was overjoyed because this was confirmation that God was responding to their prayers.

The events that took place after this fill the pages of Catherine's journals. Some of her most eloquent and penetrating writings grew out of this battle for her granddaughter's life. Considering how open and honest Catherine was with her reading public, it is surprising that she almost completely left this period of her life out of her books.

Maybe she passed over it because it was so intensely personal. At the same time, this event was a major turning point in Catherine's life that produced an abundance of visible and public fruit. She eventually emerged from this trial a spiritually mature woman, and her writing ministry was catapulted to a new level.

The following passages highlight some of the main events surrounding this precious baby:

On August 1, 1971, the second Sunday after Amy Catherine's birth, my son, after much prayer, mounted the pulpit of his East Dennis church and preached a sermon that rocked all of us. The subject was faith, and the substance of it was this:

"As you all know, my daughter Amy Catherine was born on July 22, with severe genetic problems in her liver, kidneys, and brain. The doctors have given us no hope that she will live more than a few weeks. In fact, no baby with this genetic syndrome has ever lived beyond six months. I am here to state this morning that the doctors do not have all the answers. Our Lord God does. He is the Creator of life. He decides when we are born and when we die. I do not know what His plan is for Amy Catherine. But I do know that we are to believe for her healing. In fact, right here, now, before you all and God almighty, I claim a miracle of healing for Amy Catherine."

I was sitting next to Edith during the service and felt her pride in him at that moment. Later I discovered that others in the congregation were troubled by the sermon because he'd left no loophole in case the baby died. But to me there was something very moving in the way my son stuck his chin out and said, "Lord, I believe. . . ."

What if a miraculous healing of this "hopeless" situation was part of the Spirit's mighty plan for the 1970s? Then the idea came: Call together some prayer warriors. Have them come to Cape

Cod to pray for Amy Catherine, to claim a super-natural healing![2]

Virginia Lively, a close and intimate friend of Catherine's, was one of the first of sixteen to get the call to come to Cape Cod. Miss Lively responded quickly to the crisis. As soon as she got off the phone with Catherine, she knelt down and prayed about the situation.

She knew intuitively that God desired to heal Amy Catherine, and Catherine herself told her that the Lord promised her healing if they prayed with faith. But as Miss Lively knelt there, she felt the Lord was giving her a different message: *This child will not live. But any other child they have they may have in perfect confidence.*

Virginia was startled by the Lord's words to her. How could she get a message from the Lord that was in complete contradiction to the one Catherine received? Virginia began to seriously doubt she even heard from the Lord. She wondered whether or not she should tell Catherine. When she asked the Lord to confirm the message, a flood of assurance came over her. Then she heard nothing more.

Miss Lively decided to go to Cape Cod, but not to say anything to Catherine about the message she had heard from the Lord. She was sure that He would re-veal His will to her in His own time. Nevertheless, Vir-ginia committed the Lord's words to her memory in case He opened the door for her to share them.

Meanwhile, when the group of sixteen had gath-ered at the hotel at Cape Cod, Catherine confidently told them the word she had heard from the Lord. Her

[2]*Light in My Darkest Night*, 92–93.

journal entries detail what took place as the days progressed:

> The purpose of this get-together is to pray for a miracle. The word from the Lord is that if we would gather as a group here to pray for Amy Catherine, the power of His Spirit will fall on us and Amy Catherine will be healed. . . .
>
> Something important was happening to the group through tears. . . . In fact, what we read in Scripture about how God abhors hardness of heart should convince us that tears are the sign of the hard heart melting and therefore a very true sign of the Holy Spirit.
>
> Still I went to bed that night troubled. Half of me was rejoicing over the restoration of my close relationship with the Sherrills, and over the other healings that were taking place. The other half of me was grieving over tiny Amy Catherine at the Boston hospital. Despite the massive prayer directed toward her, not only by our group of sixteen but from hundreds, perhaps thousands of people who had heard of her plight, there was no change in her condition.
>
> *What are we doing wrong, Lord?* I asked silently, staring at the ceiling. *Are we missing something? Are we so busy talking to You and to each other that we're not listening for Your instructions to us? . . .*
>
> By the third day it was obvious to all of us that the Holy Spirit had descended on our small group of sixteen. People had become painfully aware of their sins; tears of repentance were flowing, lives being redirected. To me, it was a prelude to the main event—the healing of Amy Catherine. *When,*

Lord? I kept praying. *What is Your timing? Give us Your instructions.*[3]

Indeed, extraordinary miracles were taking place among this group of prayer warriors. One of the members of the group prayed for a little girl on the same floor with Amy Catherine at Boston Children's Hospital. She was stricken with cystic fibrosis and was not expected to live. Soon after she was prayed for, she began to make a miraculous recovery.

Catherine's daughter, Linda, experienced a spiritual cleansing during her time with the group. As a result, darkness and confusion were lifted from her, and she was completely transformed. She decided to live for God rather than pursue selfish gain. This was also the beginning of healing between Catherine and Linda.

Virginia Lively was given the answer to her daughter's health problem. She had been plagued for years with symptoms of dizziness and lack of energy. No doctor was able to figure out what was causing her illness. But the Lord finally revealed to her that her daughter had a problem with low blood sugar.

A woman who had been held captive by depression for twenty years was finally freed. No amount of prayer, counseling, or psychotherapy had been able to help her. But this Cape Cod experience brought her to a place of healing, and she was restored to health.

A man's bitter resentment against his father since childhood was released by the power of prayer. A marriage was restored. Amy Catherine became a divine catalyst, a channel through which God's power was flowing into the lives of others.

This amazing prayer meeting ended with many

---

[3]Ibid., 98, 112, 124.

lives changed but with Amy Catherine still in the hospital. Catherine's journal entries detail the rest of this incredible adventure:

Our intense prayer time at Rock Harbor Manor ended on August 12. Len and I stayed another two days on the Cape, then drove to Boston to spend a day at Children's Hospital before heading back to our summer base at Evergreen Farm in Virginia. We'd been told that Amy Catherine's condition had stabilized and I took this as a sign that our prayers had begun to make a difference, that the healing had begun. . . .

To the doctor and the nurses coming in and out of the [hospital] room I must have seemed like a complete fanatic. I'm sure I was, during the whole six weeks that had now elapsed since Amy Catherine's birth. It was an all-out faith walk on my part, the most exhilarating experience of my life. If you talk about adventure, there is no adventure like totally trusting God. It was like spending six weeks walking on the water, or parachuting out of a plane, or climbing Mt. Everest.

The closest comparable experience was just after Peter Marshall's death when I was living in the kingdom of God on earth and knew with great sureness what I was to do each moment. This was different in that we were walking in blind faith. We really were. I mean, there was no sight in it—literally no way to see what lay before us. Perhaps it wasn't a faith walk at all, and we were running far ahead of the Lord. But at the time we felt we were being obedient. The highs were thrilling, the lows devastating. . . .

One such low came Friday night, September 3. Amy Catherine had had a restless day. . . . The baby's body seemed more jaundiced than usual. . . .

The mid-morning feeding went routinely. But when they began pumping the bile out of her stomach, Amy Catherine protested with cries and whimpers. I was sitting by her crib at the time, my stomach protesting, too.

After the second feeding several hours later, Amy Catherine was put into my arms while the nurse began pumping out the bile. This time Amy Catherine began crying loudly. She didn't like it at all and was telling us so. The nurse kept pumping and would not stop even when I urged her to. Suddenly her eyes darted to the heart machine. The rhythm had slowed. "I think we'd better put her back in the crib," she said, then went running for the doctor. . . .

The doctor bent over Amy Catherine for several minutes, then looked up and said gently, "The baby has expired. I'm sorry."[4]

At this point, Catherine entered into a dark night of the soul that lasted for several months. Every aspect of her life slowly started to fall apart at the seams. MGM Studios had bought the right to film *Christy*, Catherine's bestselling novel, and then had done nothing with it.

After spending years on her second novel, *Gloria*, editors convinced her to discontinue work on it. Relationships inside and outside the family were severely strained. Catherine's description of events at this point in her life is both haunting and revealing. In her own words:

> I believe that Satan won the victory last summer in the Amy Catherine situation. His handiwork is all through it. As I told the family the

---

[4]*Light in My Darkest Night*, 142, 153–155.

night before the funeral, there was a vast difference between the day of Amy Catherine's death and that of Peter Marshall back in 1949. I felt Jesus' presence in the room where Peter died. For a week after his death I walked in the glory of the kingdom of God on earth.

At the time of Amy Catherine's death, I could not feel Jesus' presence in her hospital room. On the contrary, I sensed evil there. We did not walk in any glory in the days following. Far from it! There was dissension, blame flung about, nit-picking over various decisions, a sense of failure.

Despite the good things that happened to some of the people who gathered to pray on Cape Cod, I have seen no good come from Amy Catherine's death itself. Only misunderstanding and confusion. I have not understood why the results were so negative. I have not understood what was behind all this. . . .

Inside I am dry and lonely, unable to accomplish anything, really, just going through the motions of life, barely able to do that. It is more than a dry period. I've been through those before and did not lose the Presence. This is darkness. Deadness. Awful in the way it numbs you, makes you cold and indifferent. You do the very thing, say the very word, you know you should not. Frightening!

This morning in an effort to find a handhold to pull myself out of this pit, I reread C. S. Lewis's *Screwtape Letters*. In advising the junior demon, Wormwood, how to turn Christians away from God, Screwtape warns that at times their Enemy [God] will withdraw all support from His own subjects. He continues:

"He [God] cannot 'tempt' to virtue as we do to vice. The Enemy wants them to learn to walk and must therefore take away His hand. . . . Do not be deceived, Wormwood. Our cause is never more in danger than when a human, no longer desiring, but still intending, to do our Enemy's will, looks round upon a universe from which every trace of Him seems to have vanished, and asks why he has been forsaken, and still obeys."

I find myself convicted by these words. For I know that God not only asks us to bear these dry and barren stretches of life, but even to thank Him for them. . . .

I am forced to the conclusion that Len is right. I did become spiritually arrogant after *Christy*. I became selfish with the use of my time, not wanting to be bothered with people who bored me or disagreed with me. I forgot too easily what I owed the skills of others. God was right to discipline me. I deserved it. Len was right to correct me.

But did the punishment fit the crime? I now feel so completely abandoned, rejected. The pain of Amy Catherine's death still immobilizes me. It's so dreadful to be in a state of darkness that I can understand better the fear of hell. How awful eternal darkness must be! . . .

The suffering saints—and I should include Job here, too—make my troubles seem small and paltry indeed, but their ordeals continue to frighten me. Is this the kind of "cross life" the Lord wants all of us to live? If so, why does the Bible promise in so many places "good things" for those who love the Lord? . . .

More to the point, do I have this same kind of spiritual pride and is my dark night experience His way of chastening me? I find myself with many questions and few answers. . . .

I am in rebellion against God. I have been for many months now. I am in despair about it, but

cannot seem to change. All is darkness in my life.
Nothing is working. I read books, I go to church,
Len and I pray together, but Jesus is not in any of
it.[5]

[5]Ibid., 169–170, 176, 188, 196.

8

Breakthrough

In the spring of 1972, two of Catherine's closest friends came to visit her at her Florida home. She knew they came to confront her, and, in her usual straightforward and blunt manner, Catherine told her dear friends to let her have it. She had been in seclusion battling depression for months, sickened from sleeplessness and anxiety.

Virginia and Freddie were deeply concerned for their friend and wanted desperately to help bring about something to break her out of her shell. They questioned Catherine first about her anger with God. She quickly contended that she was not angry with the Almighty, for she knew that would do no good. Then they told her that the Lord wanted her to stop wallowing in self-pity, to confess this sin of rebellion, and to repent.

Catherine immediately explained to her friends that confession and repentance had not helped:

> I've already done this, again and again. I honestly have. It's the complete lack of response that confounds me. I've never, ever lived in this kind of vacuum before. I talk, I pray. Nothing. For most

of my life I've felt God's presence, heard His voice, received thoughts that I knew came from Him. No more. He's gone from my life. I know I terribly offended Him last August. I guess I offended most everybody. But I was so totally caught up in the Amy Catherine battle. It was all-out warfare, you know. Nothing ever like it. . . .

What is destroying me is that I understand nothing about it, nothing about anything that happened. What's wrong with going all-out for something you believe in? God likes single-eyed people, doesn't He? It says so in Scripture. Well, I've always tried to be one hundred percent in everything I do. And always before, God honored my efforts. Why not this time? Why have I been flattened so completely? I know it's happened to others. Great saints have gone through dark nights a thousand times worse than mine. But they almost seemed to ask for it, seeking some higher plane of spirituality. I didn't ask for anything for myself, only that a tiny baby be healed, and God not only refused that request but turned His back on me. I don't understand.[1]

With this outpouring of Catherine's soul, Virginia was able to pinpoint the problem. She surmised that what lay at the root of Catherine's anguish was her insistence on understanding. With Virginia's words, something deep inside Catherine was moved. It was the first time in months that she had felt anything other than grief.

The next morning, much to her surprise and joy, Catherine awoke to the sound of a familiar inner voice. She felt the Lord telling her to read Isaiah 53, the prophecy of Christ's suffering and crucifixion. It

---

[1]*Light in My Darkest Night*, 199–200.

was verses 7, 9, and 10 that leaped off the pages to her:

> He was oppressed and he was afflicted, yet he never said a word. . . . He was buried like a criminal . . . but he had done no wrong. . . . Yet it was the Lord's good plan to bruise him and fill him with grief. (TLB)

The realization that God caused His own dear Son to suffer terribly and that it was a "good plan" overwhelmed Catherine. Daily she closed herself up in her room with her Bible and notebook pouring over the passages concerning Christ's sufferings. Confession and repentance flowed from her heart, which was now open to the cleansing power of the Holy Spirit.

The Lord instructed her to awake each morning at six to read His Word, to pray, and to praise Him for His goodness. One of her journal entries from this time reveals the insight the Lord was giving her:

> The word "mercy" reverberates with me. You are a merciful God. You saw my rebellion, my arrogance, and chastened me by withdrawing Your presence for a time, but You did not abandon me. Thank You, Lord, for being so loving and patient with me. The Lord is showing me this morning that my rebellion against Him following Amy Catherine's death was the central element in my sin. Rebellion was the pivotal point on which all the other unlovely qualities turned: Presumption, Hardness of heart, Self-centeredness, Self-pity, Anger, Resentment.
>
> I am beginning to see it all now. The instant we are in a state of rebellion, we have not only lost our contentment and our joy; we have also declared personal war on God. If God is truly God, then He is Lord and Ruler of circumstances. So if

we are rebellious against the circumstances He has allowed, then we are, in practical fact, rebelling against Him.

No wonder God withdrew His presence from me! My spirit of rebellion shut the door in His face. It is saying, "I will do it my way from now on. I will be the boss of my own life."

Afterward, when the darkness descends and desolation overcomes one, a few halfhearted statements like, "Well, Lord, maybe I was a bit too self-confident. . . . I guess I do need You after all. . . . Why don't we work out a sort of partnership?" These gestures won't restore the relationship. All-out repentance is needed. . . .

Thank You, Jesus, for revealing to me that to rise at six each morning is to travel from "dull sloth" to "fresh ardors." How glorious is the early morning air, the dazzling colors of the sunrise, the sweet bird sound, the fresh smell of the foliage and flowers!

Thank You, Lord, for the opportunity of this firsthand audience with the King. How privileged is that person who is admitted to the Royal Presence, to listen to the almighty King, to watch Him, to bask in His majesty. In earthly courts, such a one would be considered favored indeed. Yet this is the status and the privilege You give to each of us, Lord.[2]

Thus began Catherine's journey from darkness to light. As the weeks passed, she began to emerge from isolation and participate in daily life. Her relationship with Len was beginning to mend as they arose together each morning to worship the Lord. Honesty and truthfulness flowed between them.

---

[2]Ibid., 209–212.

It was at this time that Catherine truly came to terms with Len's divorce and let go of the animosity about it. In fact, the Lord showed Catherine how her egotism played a crucial role in her attitude toward both Amy Catherine's death and Len's divorce. She said in her journal:

> The Lord is teaching me something every day about myself. Some of it has been painful. I see ever more clearly how off-the-track I was in the summer of 1971, wanting to play God with Amy Catherine, rather than take the lower seat at the banquet table (Luke 14:7–11) and watch God in action.
>
> Now the clear insight comes to me that the undying ember underneath my guilt over marrying a divorced man is not so much that I disobeyed one of God's laws (no such lofty remorse), but rather that I have set for myself the God-playing role of always having to be right. I keep giving an order to myself subconsciously that I must never make a mistake with a major decision. It's really sheer egotism all the way. What an insight! Lord, thank You. What a fool this mortal has been.[3]

It's not that Catherine had now come to a place where she was no longer in need of trials in order to mature spiritually. She still battled fear, chronic fatigue, and weakness. There were also physical challenges such as cystic lumps and breathing difficulties. It was at this time, however, that the Lord had Catherine deal with her sleep problems. For years she had taken sleeping pills to help her insomnia. The Lord was now asking her to lay them on the altar and to trust Him to get her to sleep. With some hesitancy,

---

[3]Ibid., 242–243.

she flushed every sleeping pill down the toilet. At first,
Catherine's insomnia worsened. Every night she
would lie in bed and toss and turn for hours with no
relief. When she did finally get to sleep, Catherine
would have vivid, and sometimes disturbing, dreams.
She began to write down those dreams and determined to find out what they meant.

On September 23, 1973, the substance of her
dream was the following:

> I am the preacher's wife in a church in which
> an elaborate wedding is being solemnized—more
> gala than solemn. There are tickets to present at
> the church door and a fashion show is also to be
> part of the affair.
>
> I am acutely aware that I am not part of the
> "in" group. I seem to have arrived late and am in-
> correctly dressed. There is some discussion as to
> whether I am to be allowed into the church with-
> out a ticket. Fashionably dressed women are mill-
> ing all around me looking at me curiously.
>
> The dream ends without my knowing whether
> or not I will be admitted inside to see the cere-
> mony.[4]

Catherine recorded another dream that had to do
with being in grave danger:

> A group of us have been told that something
> important (unidentified) is missing. We are asked
> to go and get it. We have to walk a long way—up-
> hill and down, through several houses, in one
> door, out another. I feel threatened. Some of the
> women argue with me, some are belligerent.

[4]Catherine Marshall, *Something More* (New York: Guidepost Associates Inc., 1974), 87.

There are even physical threats—one especially vivid one: as we pass through one house near the front screen door, the man of the house warns, "Look out! Pull your hat over your forehead. And watch the angle that you open that door."

On the porch a rifle is mounted on a stand to the left of the door. It is connected to the door like a booby trap, so that when the door is opened to a certain angle the gun fires. I wake up shivering with fear.[5]

During this period of time, Catherine had two more dreams that were significant. She thought the Lord was trying to communicate a powerful message to her. The following is the substance of the last two dreams:

I am wandering from room to room in a large house. In the spacious dining room is a large and beautiful rug, and on it an intricately designed carved mahogany table, with portraits on the walls. An air of mustiness pervades everything as if these rooms have long been in disuse. Though I have never seen such a room, in the dream I have the impression that it is mine.

Going on to the adjoining room, I stand looking at tall cupboards with glass doors all around. They are filled with china and glassware that I recognize as belonging to me, but these possessions have not been used in a long time. I stand staring at all of it wonderingly, thinking how beautiful it is and what happiness to know that it will now be used again.

In a living room I saw a pedestal-stand about

---

[5]Ibid., 88.

two feet tall. On it had been placed the head of a woman. From a distance it looked like one of those marble busts that one sees in palaces or museums. But this bust was different. It had been severed from the body of a living woman and placed atop the pedestal.

In my dream as I looked on, a female figure appeared in the room. She looked at the bust as she passed within a few feet of it. Then she uttered just two words, "It stinks."[6]

Catherine then sought out the Reverend Morton Kelsey, a professor at Notre Dame University who was well-known for his interpretations of dreams. She asked him if he would be willing to help her. He agreed, and they set a date for a long telephone conference.

"The first thing to be done," Kelsey told her, "is to ask Jesus Christ for His power, direction, and protection." Then he gave her some general guidelines for interpreting dreams:

1. Most dream material refers to the dreamer, not the one being dreamed about.

2. The process of dreaming is in itself therapeutic.

3. One of the greatest dangers in dream interpretation is thinking that you're getting guidance for someone else.

4. When one dreams about a mate, it usually means what one is "married to" emotionally and spiritually.

Also, the general procedure for interpreting dreams:

1. Write down your dreams as soon as you awaken.

2. Write down any major events going on in your

---

[6]Ibid., 89, 96.

life at the time, including any fears or worries.

3. The more you take your dreams seriously, the more you will remember them.

4. Talk about your dreams with a trusted friend.

5. Study symbolism, analogies, and images in the Bible.

6. Pray about the dreams and ask God for the interpretation.[7]

Catherine was anxious to learn Dr. Kelsey's opinion of her dreams. The following is what he told her about the first one:

> The first one involved an elaborate wedding. How often Jesus spoke of weddings! A wedding is the union of opposites. Nothing about a real mating of opposites was possible for you until after the pill-dumping.
>
> Your dream wedding included a fashion show. It is reminiscent of the prodigal son on whom the father placed the "best robe." God is not dour or grim-visaged about His religion; His grace takes from us the burden of "oughtness" and duty, releases us to worship Him joyfully as a feast, a banquet, a celebration. When He has a wedding feast, He does it in top style!
>
> You were incorrectly dressed ... you didn't have on the right wedding garment. Remember that on September 23, you were still working through the aftermath of the pill-dumping. You were not quite ready for celebration. So the dream ended without your knowing whether you were admitted to the wedding scene.

With regard to the dream involving physical danger, Dr. Kelsey said this:

---

[7]Adapted from guidelines laid out in *Something More*, 106–108.

"We had to walk a long way," you wrote. In late September with acute insomnia still with you, the road was seeming very long indeed. The rifle on the porch is a reference to the sleeping pills, I feel sure. The dream's gun booby trap was meant to be a warning. Your victory was not yet complete. By returning to the pills you could fall back again. "Look out: Watch it! This is a life and death matter," the dream was saying. . . .

By September 30, you had won your victory, so this is a dream of promise. The house is a typical dream symbol representing one's total being.[8]

Dr. Kelsey predicted that Catherine's future work would be more significant than what she had done in the past. He also thought the "Head on the Pedestal" dream had to do with Catherine's need to understand things. He felt the dream was a warning telling her that God requires her whole being, not just her intellect.

Something about all of this rang true for Catherine. She took to heart Dr. Kelsey's interpretations, and they made a difference in her overall attitude. The darkness lifted, and she was able to once again participate in life. And the Lord blessed her abundantly. The ten years that followed this ordeal were the most productive years of her life.

Mrs. Marshall wrote five of her most penetrating books during this time. She and Len joined with John and Elizabeth Sherrill and formed a publishing company called *Chosen Books*. They published such bestsellers as *The Hiding Place* by Corrie ten Boom and *Born Again* by Chuck Colson.

For several years, Catherine and Len jointly

[8]Ibid., 108–109.

taught a class on the Christian life at their church in Delray, Florida. The church was enriched by their teaching ministry and their personal wisdom. They also helped to start the New Covenant Presbyterian Church in Pompano Beach, Florida.

In 1980 the Lord gave Catherine a vision of a ministry of intercessory prayer. *Breakthrough*, an outreach that brings together those in need with those who want to pray for those in desperate situations, was the fruit of this vision. She also developed a periodical newsletter in order to teach about intercessory prayer and to share fresh insights about it.

One such insight had to do with servanthood. The Lord had given Catherine a vision of the need for the body of Christ to serve one another for His glory. But she also saw in a new and fresh way the servant role that the Lord himself wants to play in the lives of His servants. Her discovery was this:

> The message I am getting today from Jesus is the servant role that He wants to play in the lives of every one of us. Scriptures that affirm this include Matthew 20:28: "The Son of man came not to be waited on but to serve, and to give His life as a ransom for many"; and Luke 22:27: "I am in your midst as one who serves."
>
> When Jesus wrapped a towel around His waist, poured water into the basin, and began to wash His disciples' feet (see John 13:4–5), Simon Peter objected that this was beneath the dignity of the Master. I want to insist along with Peter that we, as His disciples and intercessors today, are to be the servants.
>
> But Jesus answered him, "If I do not wash you, you have no part in me." This is a stunning and stupendous thought. Unless I can believe in this

much love for me, unless I can and will accept Him
with faith as my Servant as well as my God, unless I truly know that it is my good He seeks, not
His glory (He already has all of that He can use
for all eternity), then I cannot have His companionship. What an amazing revelation![9]

Catherine realized that the Lord had been prepar-
ing her all along for this kind of prayer ministry. She
had been interceding for loved ones since the early
days of Peter Marshall's ministry, culminating in the
battle for Amy Catherine's life. What she learned first
and foremost from these experiences was patience.
The following is a petition for patience, which she offered regularly for those she interceded for:

Lord Jesus, You want honest words on my lips;
no thought of mine is hidden from You anyway. I
am puzzled about the Father's timing. You know
how long I have been praying for ———.

I have tried to be patient about the answer. I
know that the seasons come and go in majestic se-
quence. The earth rotates on its axis in a pre-
determined rhythm. No prayers of mine could
change any of this. I know that Your ways are not
my ways; Your timing is not my timing. But Lord,
how do I, so earthbound, come to terms with the
pace of eternity?

I want to be teachable, Lord. Is there something You want to show me, some block You want
removed, some change You want in me or in my
attitudes before You can answer prayer? Give me
the gift of eyes that see, of ears that hear what You
are saying to me.

Come, Lord Jesus, and abide in my heart. How

grateful I am to realize that the answer to my prayer does not depend on me at all! As I quietly abide in You and let Your life flow into me, what freedom it is to know that the Father does not see my threadbare patience or insufficient trust, rather only Your patience, Lord, and Your confidence that the Father has everything in hand. In Your faith I thank You right now for a more glorious answer than I can imagine. Amen.[10]

The Lord not only blessed Catherine's ministry, but He also restored to her the years the locusts had eaten (see Joel 2:25). On May 4, 1974, her daughter-in-law, Edith, gave birth to Peter Jonathan Marshall, a perfectly healthy baby boy. On September 24, 1980, Peter and Edith welcomed David Christopher Marshall, another healthy baby boy, into their family.

Virginia Lively's prophecies had come to pass. The Lord had showed her just before Amy Catherine's death that the Marshalls could have perfect confidence in the health of their future babies. And everyone, especially Grandma Marshall, rejoiced in God's goodness. About the momentous occasions, Catherine wrote:

> Goodness and mercy shall follow you all the days of your life. This had been His pledge to me on that dark day of Peter Marshall's death as I was about to leave the little hospital room with my life lying in shambles about me. "Goodness and mercy." . . . His goodness. His mercy. How bounteously He has honored His pledge to me. Sometimes we have to lift our eyes to the hills to get His perspective, wait for what seems to us earthbound creatures a long time to see the ful-

---

[10]Ibid., 301–302.

fillment of His promises. But this I have learned—
we can trust Him.[11]

Though Catherine had learned to trust the Lord
with total abandonment and had firmly placed her
feet on the solid rock of faith, doubts about His presence still crept into her heart on occasion. In her latter
years, Catherine's doubts manifested themselves in
fear. And this fear reached its highest point in the fear
of death.

---

[11]*Meeting God at Every Turn*, 251.

9

The Twilight Years

On August 18, 1979, the LeSourd and Marshall families gave Catherine and Len a surprise twentieth wedding anniversary party, which lasted almost an entire weekend. Their actual anniversary date was November 14, but the summer was the only time the entire family was able to join together.

The event took place at the Marshall Evergreen Farm in Virginia, where Len and Catherine had often spent summers with Catherine's parents. After her father's death, Catherine's mother moved to Florida to live with them. At the time of the celebration, Peter and Edith lived next door to Len and Catherine.

The two families arrived at the farm a week before the party. On the special night, Len and Catherine were instructed to wear their finest clothes and to wait in their bedroom until they were summoned. At approximately 6:40 P.M., their grandchildren, Mary Elizabeth and Peter Jonathan, came and escorted them to the living room where the rest of the family was waiting. Chester then read from a scroll these words:

Hear ye, Hear ye, Hear ye.

Sarah Catherine Wood Marshall LeSourd
and
Leonard Earle LeSourd

having been joined in holy matrimony,
lo, these 20 years,
it is only fitting and proper that
this august occasion be set aside
to honor your union and its subsequent fruits.
Heretofore, be it known that the undersigned
do express their heartfelt gratitude and admiration,
acknowledge their overwhelming debt,
and pledge their loyalty, love, and service.

Delivered this 18th day of August, 1979, by

Leonora Whitaker Wood	Leonard Chester LeSourd
Edith Wallis Marshall	Jeffrey Allan LeSourd
Peter John Marshall	Mary Elizabeth Marshall
Linda Ann LeSourd	Peter Jonathan Marshall[1]

The families then escorted Catherine and Len to the dining room and served them their favorite meal. It was an evening filled with all kinds of festivities, one Catherine would surely never forget. The evening culminated with a request for the LeSourds to "tell all" about their meeting and courtship. Even the grandchildren were anxious to hear the story!

As Catherine sat there reveling in these precious moments, her mind wandered back to something she originally wrote in 1961, two years after their marriage. In the foreword of her book *Beyond Our Selves*, she wrote,

Len's three children have joined Peter John in

---

[1]*Meeting God at Every Turn*, 236–237.

calling me "Mother." Many experiences have tested me in my lifetime, but none more than this one. And none has made me happier. But writing about it must come later. A man swimming a horse across a turbulent stream does not stop to take a picture of the experience. I'll get my colts across the stream, see them thoroughly dried off, well fed and on their way—then perhaps, the picture.[2]

She realized right then that "the colts" had made it safely across the stream and were now joyously ministering to the ones who got them there. This was truly one of the most special moments of her life. The members of her family were healthy and secure, and, most importantly, they were all walking with the Lord. Catherine graciously thanked the One who had made it all possible.

It was about this same time that Catherine made a rather odd confession to Len. She told him that she feared death. She had been dwelling on this because of her recent battles with emphysema. She had been severely weakened by this disease and sensed that her time on earth would soon draw to a close.

This confession took Len completely by surprise. In recent years, Catherine had written quite extensively on the subject of the afterlife and seemed to be comfortable with it. So the thought of her fearing immortality did not make any sense to him. However, she was not talking about a fear of immortality, but a fear of death itself.

Since childhood, Catherine always felt that death was the ultimate enemy—something to be defied and

---

[2]*Beyond Our Selves*, reprint. ed. (Grand Rapids, Mich.: Fleming H. Revell, 1994), xvi-xvii.

overcome. To "give in" to the idea of death would be to admit defeat, something she was not willing to do. In response, Len spent hours in prayer about Catherine's fear. As the spiritual head, he was not about to let Satan, the real Enemy, get the best of his wife.

By 1982 Catherine was so weakened by emphysema that she could hardly work. Every morning she would go into her office at home and make an attempt to get something done, but a short while later she would go back to her bedroom, exhausted and defeated by her physical condition. But Len constantly encouraged Catherine to stay true to her battling nature and not give up. And every night he anointed her with oil, taking a stand against her illness.

During this time, Catherine experienced further spiritual transformation. She was first of all concerned about the Lord's unfinished work in her, especially as it pertained to her fear of death. She picked up a biography on John Wesley and found that he, too, had this concern. Outwardly he lived a life of confident devotion to God; inwardly, however, Wesley still feared death. That is, until he had a personal experience with the Holy Spirit. Only then was he assured that Christ had a place for him in heaven.

But this was still unfinished business to Catherine. Then she realized why this was so. She had not yet offered her body to Him as a *living* sacrifice. Only then could she be free from the fear of death.

One day, at precisely 4:40 P.M., Catherine offered herself to Him unconditionally—to obey Him hour by hour, day by day, regardless of the circumstances. She was at that point willing to be "crucified with Christ." Shortly thereafter, breathlessness overtook her, and her energy level dropped so low that she could hardly walk.

On July 9, 1982, Catherine was taken to the hospital. She spent thirty-two days in the intensive care unit. The carbon dioxide level in her body was very high, and the prognosis was not good. Soon after her arrival there, the Lord reminded Catherine of her commitment to Him to offer herself as a living sacrifice (Romans 12:1).

On July 24, fifteen days into her stay at the hospital, the Lord took her through a crucifixion experience. She described in detail what happened in those few moments:

> While lying on my back, hour after hour, unable to read or talk, I had plenty of time to reflect on the study I did awhile ago on the "Humanity of Jesus." Through it I saw that His humanness for thirty-three years on earth was real; that He was as helpless, as "out of control" of circumstances, as we are. All this was in order for Him to be the Way-shower, the true and very practical Captain of our salvation. I also perceived that during this earthly walk, the guiding principle of Jesus' life was "what pleases My Father in heaven, never what I want to do."
>
> In the intervening months since I made this study, several things have been happening: (1) The Holy Spirit has been doing a steady softening and melting process within me. This has meant that the plights of other persons presented to me, mostly through correspondence, have been laid on my heart with a new urgency; (2) During this same period my own circumstances have not only been taken out of my control, but also have gone in directions contrary to anything I would wish.
>
> At what point in the Christian walk are we actually "crucified with Him"? At what point is the moral self dead on His cross and buried with Him?

In my case, I concluded, dying to self has been going on for some time. For me, it has been a slow, torturous, lingering death indeed—no doubt because I have been resisting all the way. I'm reasonably sure that it need not be this drawn out and this painful, if the believer really understands what is going on and why, and assents to it in his will. Yet I do think it's something we have to walk through all the way and feel. Death on a cross hurts.

Early on the morning of July 24, the climax came for me. I was in a semiconscious, dreaming state, when I felt myself literally hanging on the cross with Jesus. There was no pain from the nails in my hands or feet; only a suffocating, crushing weight on my chest as my entire body dragged downward. I knew I was close to death, but strangely there was absolutely no fear.

As the weight on the rib cage grew unendurable, however, I was aware of a dark presence, as well as that of Jesus. A fierce struggle with some evil force ensued. Again and again, I rebuked the dark power and ordered him to be gone. He didn't leave easily, but leave he did at last.

Then—so gently—Jesus picked me up and removed me from the cross. As He did so, three words came to me: "The Great Exchange." Later I realized this is what theologians call "the substitutionary atonement," meaning that every sinful thing in our lives was dealt with in Christ's finished work on His Cross. At the moment, I knew only that the crushing weight had lifted from my ribs.[3]

---

[3]Catherine Marshall, *The Inspirational Writings of Catherine Marshall: A Closer Walk* (Corvallis, Ore.: Arrowwood Press, 1991), 491–492.

At that point, Catherine felt that a miracle had taken place in her body. The doctors confirmed that the carbon dioxide levels had dropped as mysteriously as they had increased. The prognosis, which originally was that she would never come off the respirator, was now much more positive. By August 11 all the tubes in her body were removed. On August 20 she was released from the hospital.

Nevertheless, Catherine was still very sick. She had lost twenty-five pounds in the ICU, and the recuperation process was expected to last several months. Discouragement quickly set in as Catherine was helpless to accomplish anything. Her pastor, Robert Bonham, was a great help to her at this time. He told her she going through the grief process.

During her hospital stay, he pointed out, she experienced a great deal of loss: a loss of identity, a loss of dignity, a loss of speech, and a loss of mental ability. These were slowly being restored to her in the recovery process; but the experience of loss is still the same. She must now grieve through them.

Something deep within Catherine's spirit confirmed the truth of her pastor's insights. So she walked through the grieving process willingly. Besides the losses pointed out to her by her pastor, she also experienced a loss of "importance" as she realized that the world went on quite well without her.

But there was rejoicing in this grieving period as well. Catherine realized that for the first time in her life she no longer feared death. This was one loss she would not miss. The Lord had finally broken her chains of fear and set her free to look forward to the future with Him.

With all of this behind her, Catherine was able to receive love from others as she was never able to do before. Through this, the Lord was bringing about Catherine's healing from the inside out. She finally realized that what was missing from her 1944 experience of Jesus' healing presence was not faith, but love.

She had now come to a place where she could receive the love of others. And the strength and healing that flowed from the love of family and friends overwhelmed her. "Lord, I rejoice," she wrote in her journal. "Lord, let Your love—and Len's, and the love of those around me, each member of my family, and all the love of far-flung friends through my books—*take over*."[4]

At the beginning of 1983, Catherine resumed her writing ministry. An eight-hundred-page draft of *Julie* had been completed but still required much work to refine characterization. She had several article ideas for the *Intercessors* newsletter and the *Guideposts* magazine.

However, at the end of January, Catherine had to undergo cataract surgery. Shortly thereafter, her health started to fail again. The following are her last journal entries:

February 9th: I am staggering under what the eye surgeon said to me yesterday during a routine checkup following the cataract surgery: "You are sick from head to toe." I did not have to accept this verdict, but I did. Now I really have to ditch it—with the Spirit's help and by God's grace. This verse has truly helped me:

"And if the Spirit of Him Who raised up Jesus from the dead dwells in you, [then] He Who raised up Jesus from the dead will also restore to life your mortal (short-lived, perishable) bodies

4Ibid., 500.

through His Spirit Who dwells in you" (Romans 8:11, Amplified).

February 24th: Have hit a new low. I am quite out of breath—indeed, gasping for air—just in walking from room to room. My doctor could find no obvious cause for the trouble yesterday. Today it hit me. . . . Once again the doctors neither know what is wrong, nor how to help me. So . . . I am backed up against Jesus' help.

March 9th: In my Quiet Time, this thought: my hospital experience of the crucifixion was centered on the matter of breathing. This morning the Holy Spirit reminded me once again: "Jesus took your breathing problem into His own body on the Cross so that from henceforth He is your life-breath."

(Catherine was admitted to the hospital on March 11 for more tests.)

March 12th: The blood test yesterday showed carbon dioxide level in my blood too high, but not dangerous; not enough oxygen in the blood, however. Another problem seems to be anemia. This morning Jesus told me once again: "Keep your eyes off yourself and look steadily at Me. I love you. I know how to mend you."[5]

And Jesus did mend her—eternally. On March 18, 1983, shortly after midnight, at sixty-nine years of age, Catherine Marshall breathed her last on earth and went home to be with her Lord. There is little doubt that there was much rejoicing in heaven when Catherine and Jesus met each other face-to-face.

But here on earth the family grieved the loss of

[5]Ibid., 510–511.

such a tremendous woman. The funeral service took place at National Presbyterian Church in Washington, D.C. She was buried next to her late first husband, Peter Marshall, and her two deceased grandchildren, Peter Christopher and Amy Catherine.

A memorial service was also given at the New Covenant Presbyterian Church in Pompano Beach, Florida, where she fellowshiped for years. Her pastor and good friend Robert Bonham spoke these moving words at her service:

> During Catherine's funeral in the National Presbyterian Church, my eyes went to some beautiful stained-glass windows through which the sun was shining. I thought of Jesus telling His disciples, "You are the light of the world." Catherine, as a twentieth-century follower, put her light on a lampstand so that all might see.
>
> I looked at the glass in those windows and thought about all the pieces therein. There were dark pieces and light pieces, all kinds of colors blended together. I thought about the suffering experiences that Catherine had early in her life and recently in the hospital. These were deep, deep colors. Her body never was able to keep up with her mind and her spirit. It always hauled her back.
>
> There were, of course, the brighter colors, the rose tints of love and warmth—the giving of her heart to those in her family and to everyone she touched. Those colors went out across the United States and throughout the world. I remember years back when I was at the University of Illinois, one of the professors there had a hydrocephalic child. He told me that he had called Catherine up long-distance and had asked her to pray for his child. She did, and the child was healed. All

the way to Illinois, and other places far and near, went those pieces of radiating light—warm, bright, healing colors falling on the lives of people.

There were so many pieces in her life—the books that she and the Lord wrote—the articles for *Guideposts* and other magazines. She wrote nothing that did not have all of her heart and mind in it as well as the heart and mind of Christ. Starting *The Intercessors* not long ago, she and Leonard mobilized prayer warriors across the nation to bring help to many people. Her family represents warm, glowing pieces of glass in the mosaic of her life. Likewise her many friends who kept calling when she died and could not believe that this had happened.

A surprising thing about a stained-glass window is that when the light does not shine through, it comes across as dull. Have you ever looked at a stained-glass window when there is no light behind it? You cannot see what is in it. Catherine always had Christ's light shining through her life. As the light of Jesus radiated through the stained-glass mosaic of her life, all of us who were within sight of it got blessed.

When the sun goes down, the horizon stays bright for a long time. There is going to be a long afterglow to Catherine Marshall LeSourd's life. The books that were written will go on to become classics in Christian literature. The articles will go on helping people. There are things she has written that will yet find their way into print to bless us. Her touches on our lives will live on, ministering to my children, and my children's children.[6]

Pastor Bonham went on to quote the last page of

---

[6] Ibid., 512–513.

her book *To Live Again*, where she wrote about facing life without Peter. She discussed her assurance that God would be in her future even as He was in her past, bringing new adventures and new hope. She affirmed that she would move steadily toward His Light—no matter what. And that is exactly what she did.

Appendix I

Catherine's Lifeline to God

Catherine Marshall was neither seminary-trained, nor was she ever a part of the clergy. Yet few could deny that she was very well-versed in the Scriptures and in many aspects of orthodox Christian theology. She ministered to thousands around the world through her writing and speaking career.

The previous chapters have shown that at the center of all Catherine's endeavors, from the mundane to the sacred, God was there. Her life experiences constantly drove her to the fountain of living waters, which became her source of spiritual strength.

Mrs. Marshall did not write a systematic theological treatise per se; but she did leave behind a rich storehouse of intimate memoirs and personal Bible studies. Because these topics were so vitally important to her life and her ministry, the following is an attempt to outline what she believed about the Trinity, Satan, spiritual growth, and the Bible.

While some of these things have been discussed in previous chapters, it would be beneficial to understand the full spectrum of Catherine's theological beliefs.

(1) Catherine believed the Holy Spirit did not limit His revelations to the truths contained in the Old and New Testaments. She based this belief on John 16:12–13: "I have much more to say to you, more than you can now bear. But when he, the Spirit of truth, comes, he will guide you into all truth. He will not speak on his own; he will speak only what he hears, and he will tell you what is yet to come" (NIV).

She held that God always has some new spiritual insight for each believer—not something contrary to Scripture, but something that applies to the individual in accordance with revealed truth.

(2) She also believed God was in everything, whether it was good or evil. This, of course, was the hard lesson she learned in the wake of the death of her granddaughter Amy Catherine. With respect to the problem of evil, Hanna Whitall Smith's book *The Christian's Secret of a Happy Life* had a tremendous impact on her. Catherine read this book during her first major illness back in the '40s.

Smith argued that unless we accepted "everything" as coming directly from the hand of God, we could never know true contentment. She wrote,

> What is needed is to see God in everything, and to receive everything directly from His hands, with no intervention of second causes. . . . An earthly parent's care for his helpless child is a feeble illustration of this. If the child is in its father's arms, nothing can touch it without that father's consent, unless he is too weak to prevent it. And even if this should be the case, he suffers the harm first in his own person before he allows it to reach the child. If an earthly parent could thus care for his little helpless one, how much more will our

Heavenly Father! . . .[1]

Catherine rejected this notion for twenty-seven years. Finally, though, she grew to accept the divine hand in everything, learning that relinquishment is the doorway to praise. Hence, the sovereignty of God became one of the major cornerstones of her faith. To go along with this, Mrs. Marshall also held tenaciously to the mercy, goodness, and love of God.

(3) Being a Spirit-filled, Spirit-led Christian, Catherine did not take spiritual warfare lightly. Accordingly, she believed it was essential that every Christian be prepared to battle his or her Enemy, the devil. Her study of the Scriptures on this subject and her personal experience led her to list the following antithetical goals of Jesus and Satan.

Satan	Jesus
Seeks to do his own will.	Always obeys His Father's will.
Aims to bind and blind men.	Yearns to free men and open their eyes to see.
Lies interminably.	Is the Truth.
Takes himself very seriously, cannot bear taunting or levity.	Often uses the light touch.
Wants us to live in darkness and hide portions of our life from others.	Wants us to live in the light.
Wants us to doubt and disbelieve God's Word.	Longs for us to have faith that He always keeps His Word.
Works to make us ignore, disbelieve, or choose for ourselves what to believe in the Scripture.	Steadily assures us that the Scripture is the Word of God.

---

[1]Hanna Whitall Smith, *The Christian's Secret of a Happy Life* (Westwood, N.J.: Fleming H. Revell Co., 1962), 144, 146.

Pushes us to disobey God.	Says, "If you love Me, you will obey My commandments."
Urges us to use God for selfish purposes.	Longs that we be used by God to help others.
Tells us, "Your body belongs to you."	Tells us, "Your body is the temple of the Holy Spirit."
Wants sickness and disease.	Wants wholeness of body, mind, and spirit.
Spares no effort to bring us sorrow and grief.	Wants our joy.
Desires our death.	Eagerly bestows life stretching on into eternity.
Condemns and accuses us.	Assures us, "I came not to judge the world, but to save the world."
Pushes us toward selfish contempt.	Assures us that each man is of infinite worth to Him.
Fosters discontent and grumbling.	Urges contentment and praise in all situations.
Urges us to think that we can get virtue for life in an instant.	Desires that we depend on Him minute by minute for what we need and claim our "daily bread."
Urges us to concentrate on the sins of others.	Tells us to look at the beam in our own eye and remove that first.
Wants us to hang onto resentment and bitterness.	Tells us to forgive others in the same ways God forgives us.
Urges us to have fun now, try to forget about paying for it.	Influences us to pay now in time and effort, then fun later is assured.
Attempts to get us to hide our sins and make excuses for them, thus encouraging their festering within.	Wishes us to run to Him, bring our sins into the light, and have them forgiven, cleansed, and forgotten.
Labors to have us believe that temptation is sin.	Assures us that temptation rightly handled strengthens us.

Wants us, when we fail, to wallow in discouragement or despair.	Encourages us in failure to ask forgiveness, accept it, rise, and go on.
Aims for us always to wear a mask and act a part; to be all things to all people.	Plants in us a desire to be true to ourselves; to let others know where we stand.
Wants our faith always to be for the future.	Wants us to cultivate a present moment faith.
Seeks steady procrastination.	Teaches us that "now is the day of salvation."
Strives to have us preoccupied with "what ifs?" (what might happen); to be plagued with thoughts of the future.	Is concerned with what we do in the present; wants us to offer up the present moment to God.
Urges us toward a false, lofty superspirituality.	Wants us to live out a daily "without Me ye can do nothing."
Delights in a moderate religion with no extremes.	Wants the total man—"Thou shalt love the Lord your God with all your heart and with all your soul and with all your mind."
Works for churches to be divided into "clubs" or factions with "party spirit."	Leads us toward unity amid diversity of gifts of the Spirit among the people in the church.
Wants us to see all morality as relative, no final truth or falsehood.	Insists that He is the Way, the Truth and the Life; God's laws are absolute.
Labors to destroy all law, God's and man's.	Fulfills the law and the prophets and adds righteousness to it.
Labors for war.	Desires peace, the fruit of righteousness.[2]

According to Catherine, God has given believers at least three defense tactics to escape the temptations brought on by Satan. The first is the freedom of choice.

[2]*Something More*, 133–136.

While we do not always make good decisions, God has given believers the power and grace to consistently choose to live according to His pattern for us. Therefore, we must choose to submit to Him daily.

The second weapon God has given us is the "armor of light." That is, as long as we are transparent, honest, and refuse to keep any dark secrets, Satan will leave us alone. He flees from those whose walk is consistent with Christlikeness and whose heart's desire is to live in His light.

The third tactic, according to Catherine, is offensive rather than defensive. It is the truth as it is found in Scripture. A believer who takes a stand on God's Word will have little trouble with the Enemy. "It is written" was the phrase Jesus used against Satan while in the wilderness, and that same power is available to His followers in all generations.

(4) Catherine's theology on spiritual growth is the most comprehensive aspect of her belief system. Besides the Bible, she was greatly influenced by many Christian stalwarts of the past. She read books by A. B. Simpson, Frank C. Laubach, C. S. Lewis, and Agnes Sanford. She diligently studied the personal journals and letters of Brother Lawrence, John Foxe, John Wesley, Hanna Whitall Smith, George Muller, and Evelyn Underhill.

Catherine set the personal experience of these strong Christians alongside the New Testament and began to see some similarities. She discovered, first of all, that the "experiential approach" had some precedent in the Bible. Jesus proved He was the Messiah not by His theology per se, but by His miracles. And most of those miracles involved healing.

Healing occupied Catherine's mind most of her Christian life. She knew God had the power to heal and that He wanted to heal. The fact that He did not heal all the time puzzled her to no end. This is why she experienced a crisis of faith at the death of her baby granddaughter.

After this tragedy, Catherine discovered the key that not only helped her to come to terms with the enigma of healing, but also opened the door to spiritual growth, as well. Relinquishment, Mrs. Marshall contended, keeps the believer on the path of discipleship and on the road to Christlikeness. Nothing pleases the heart of God more than His children's complete dependence on Him.

Relinquishment is the umbrella under which the entire process of spiritual growth takes place. Relinquishment means the giving up of one's will and one's need to understand. Obedience, joy, contentment, forgiveness, and praise are simply not possible without first laying aside one's desire to have things one's own way.

The need to understand was a huge stumbling block for Catherine. Her self-will also kept her on many occasions from experiencing God's peace. For instance, when she prayed for Amy Catherine's healing, she assumed it was God's will to heal her. When the baby died, Catherine insisted on understanding why she wasn't healed.

After months of searching for answers, she laid her need to understand on the altar. This act of relinquishment taught her that self-will, presumption, and the need to understand put her in a place of authority that only God has a right to hold. There is only one God, and only He has the authority to do and to say what will happen when.

She also discovered that we are never more like the devil than when we attempt to be like God in this way.

He lures us to take the place of judgment and to rely on our limited knowledge of good and evil. Speaking from personal experience, Catherine argues that rebellion reaches its pinnacle in all such attitudes. And God simply will not tolerate this kind of arrogance from us. Relinquishment is the only way to be freed from our pursuit of godhood. For Catherine, Christ was the supreme example of a life lived in complete dependence upon God. It took her practically to the end of her life to realize this precious truth. But when she finally did, every ounce of her energy was spent in trying to follow in her Master's steps.

All of this taken together represents Catherine's view of spiritual growth. She emphasized the place of the Holy Spirit in the life of the believer, holding that there could be no growth or insight without Him. By dreams and visions, along with the Scriptures and other believers, the Spirit leads the individual into a deeper knowledge of Jesus.

As with so many aspects of her belief system, Catherine's view of spiritual growth came from the Scriptures as well as from her own personal experiences. For Catherine, dreams and visions had just as much spiritual authority as the Bible. As we have seen, they played an extremely important role in her life.

(5) For many years, Catherine began each day with an open Bible, an open notebook, and an open heart. God's Word was an integral part of her everyday life. She believed with all her heart that one could not know God unless one first knew His Word. The Scriptures provided her with the spiritual strength she needed to make it through her hectic days.

The Bible was Catherine's mainstay through her many bouts with illness. She expected that God would speak to her specifically in His Word, and He did. He gave her insight not only about spiritual things, but about the mundane, as well. She learned from this that God is concerned about every aspect of life. She once wrote:

> The God I know does not want us to divide life up into compartments—"this is spiritual, so this is God's providence, but that part over there is physical, so I'll have to handle that myself." If we are to believe Jesus, [then] His Father and our Father is the God of all life, and His caring and provision include a sheepherder's lost lamb, a falling sparrow, a sick child, the hunger pangs of a crowd of thousands, the need for wine at a wedding feast, and the plight of professional fishermen who toiled all night and caught nothing. These vignettes, scattered through the Gospels like little patches of gold dust, say to us, "No creaturely need is outside the scope or range of prayer."[3]

Needless to say, prayer was absolutely essential in the life of Catherine Marshall. She wrote quite extensively on the topic; but, most importantly, she lived a life of prayer. The following is her life-changing prayer of relinquishment:

> Father, for such a long time I have pleaded before You this, the deep desire of my heart: _____.
> Yet the more I've clamored for Your help with this, the more remote You have seemed.
> I confess my demanding spirit in this matter. I've tried suggesting to You ways my prayer could be answered. To my shame, I've even bargained with You. Yet I know that trying to manipulate the Lord of the universe is utter foolishness. No won-

---

[3]*The Inspirational Writings of Catherine Marshall*, 191.

der my spirit is so sore and weary!

I want to trust You, Father. My spirit knows that these verities are forever trustworthy even when I feel nothing. . . .

That You are there. (You said, "Lo, I am with you always.")

That You love me. (You said, "I have loved you with an everlasting love.")

That You alone know what is best for me. (For in You, Lord, are hidden all the treasures of wisdom and knowledge.)

Perhaps all along, You have been waiting for me to give up self-effort. At last I want You in my life even more than I want _____ . So now, by an act of my will, I relinquish this to You. I will accept Your will, whatever that may be. Thank You for counting this act of my will as the decision of the real person even when my emotions protest. I ask You to hold me true to this decision. To You, Lord God, who alone are worthy of worship, I bend the knee with thanksgiving that this, too, will "work together for good." Amen.[4]

For years Catherine copied Bible verses in her notebook that helped her during times of health or household crises(The following forty-one verses became Catherine's scriptural lifeline in times of trouble:)

"Behold, I am the Lord, the God of all flesh: is there any thing too hard for me?" (Jeremiah 32:27 KJV).

"The grass withers, the flowers fade, but the word of our God will stand forever" (Isaiah 40:8 NRSV).

"He has bestowed on us His precious and exceed-

[4]Catherine Marshall, *Adventures in Prayer*, reprint. ed. (Grand Rapids, Mich.: Chosen Books, 1985), 60.

ingly great promises, so that through them you may escape (by flight) from the moral decay (rottenness and corruption) that is in the world because of covetousness (lust and greed), and become sharers (partakers) of the divine nature" (2 Peter 1:4 AMPLIFIED).

"God is faithful—reliable, trustworthy and [therefore] ever true to His promise, and He can be depended on; by Him you were called into companionship and participation with His Son, Jesus Christ our Lord" (1 Corinthians 1:9 AMPLIFIED).

"So shall my word be that goeth forth out of my mouth: it shall not return unto me void, but it shall accomplish that which I please, and it shall prosper in the thing whereto I sent it" (Isaiah 55:11 KJV).

"And if the Spirit of Him Who raised Jesus from the dead dwells in you, [then] He Who raised up Christ Jesus from the dead will also restore to life your mortal (short-lived, perishable) bodies through His Spirit Who dwells in you" (Romans 8:11 AMPLIFIED).

"So too the (Holy) Spirit comes to our aid and bears us up in our weakness; for we do not know what prayer to offer nor how to offer it worthily as we ought, but the Spirit Himself goes to meet our supplication and pleads in our behalf with unspeakable yearnings and groanings too deep for utterance" (Romans 8:26 AMPLIFIED).

"And we know that all things work together for good to them that love God, to them who are the called according to his purpose" (Romans 8:28 KJV).

"I know that, whatsoever God doeth, it shall be for ever: nothing can be put to it, nor anything taken from it: and God doeth it, that men should fear before him" (Ecclesiastes 3:14 KJV).

"(For the Lord is our Judge, the Lord is our Lawgiver, the Lord is our King; He will save us)" (Isaiah 33:22 NKJV).

"For I, the Lord your God, hold your right hand; I, Who say to you, Fear not, I will help you!" (Isaiah 41:13 AMPLIFIED).

"For God's gifts and His call are irrevocable—He never withdraws them when once they are given, and He does not change His mind about those to whom He gives His grace or to whom He sends His call" (Romans 11:29 AMPLIFIED).

"When the enemy shall come in like a flood, the Spirit of the Lord will lift up a standard against him and put him to flight—for He will come like a rushing stream which the breath of the Lord drives" (Isaiah 59:19 AMPLIFIED).

"But God is faithful [to His Word and to His compassionate nature], and He [can be trusted] not to let you be tempted . . . beyond your ability and strength of resistance. . . . He will [always] also provide the way out—the means of escape to a landing place—that you may be capable and strong and powerful patiently to bear up under it" (1 Corinthians 10:13 AMPLIFIED).

"The Lord redeems the life of His servants, and none of those who take refuge and trust in Him shall be condemned or held guilty" (Psalm 34:22 AMPLIFIED).

"Though I walk in the midst of trouble, You will revive me; You will stretch forth Your hand against the wrath of my enemies, and Your right hand will save me" (Psalm 138:7 AMPLIFIED).

"And He will establish you to the end—keep you steadfast, give you strength, and guarantee you vindication, that is, be your warrant against all accusation or indictment—[so that you will be] guiltless and irreproachable in the day of our Lord Jesus Christ, the

Messiah" (1 Corinthians 1:8 AMPLIFIED).

"He will swallow up death in victory—He will abolish death forever; and the Lord God will wipe away tears from off all faces; and the reproach of His people He will take away from off all the earth; for the Lord has spoken it" (Isaiah 25:8 AMPLIFIED).

"Fear not . . . for I am with you; do not . . . be dismayed, for I am your God. I will strengthen and harden you [to difficulties]; yes, I will help you; yes, I will hold you up and retain you with My victorious right hand of rightness and justice" (Isaiah 41:10 AMPLIFIED).

"I have called you by your name; You are Mine. When you pass through the waters, I will be with you; And through the rivers, they shall not overflow you. When you walk through the fire, you shall not be burned, nor shall the flame scorch you. For I am the Lord your God, the Holy One of Israel, your Savior . . ." (Isaiah 43:1–3 NKJV).

"For thus saith the Lord God, the Holy One of Israel; 'In returning and rest shall ye be saved; in quietness and in confidence shall be your strength' " (Isaiah 30:15 KJV).

"In the world you have tribulation and trials and distress and frustration; but be of good cheer—take courage, be confident, certain, undaunted—for I have overcome the world.—I have deprived it of power to harm, have conquered it [for you]" (John 16:33 AMPLIFIED).

"I assure you, most solemnly I tell you, the person whose ears are open to My words—who listens to My message—and believes and trusts in and clings to and relies on Him Who sent Me has (possesses now) eternal life. And he does not come into judgment—does not incur sentence of judgment, will not come under condemnation—but he has already passed over out of death into life" (John 5:24 AMPLIFIED).

"Do not fret or have any anxiety about anything, but in every circumstance and in everything by prayer and petition [definite requests] with thanksgiving continue to make your wants known to God. And God's peace . . . which transcends all understanding, shall garrison and mount guard over your hearts and minds in Christ Jesus" (Philippians 4:6–7 AMPLIFIED).

"But they that wait upon the Lord shall renew their strength; they shall mount up with wings as eagles; they shall run, and not be weary; and they shall walk, and not faint" (Isaiah 40:31 KJV).

"Whoever drinks of the water that I will give him shall never, no never, be thirsty any more. But the water that I will give him shall become a spring of water welling up (flowing, bubbling) continually within him unto (into, for) eternal life" (John 4:14 AMPLIFIED).

"My sheep hear my voice, and I know them, and they follow me: And I give unto them eternal life; and they shall never perish, neither shall any man pluck them out of my hand. My Father, which gave them me, is greater than all; and no man is able to pluck them out of my Father's hand. I and my Father are one" (John 10:27–30 KJV).

"Keep and protect me, O God, for in You I have found refuge, and in You do I put my trust and hide myself. . . . My body too shall rest and confidently dwell in safety" (Psalm 16:1, 9 AMPLIFIED).

"In the day when I called, You answered me, and strengthened me with strength (might and inflexibility) [to temptation] in my inner self" (Psalm 138:3 AMPLIFIED).

"Now the Lord is the Spirit, and where the Spirit

of the Lord is, there is liberty—emancipation from bondage, freedom" (2 Corinthians 3:17 AMPLIFIED).

"(For the weapons of our warfare are not carnal, but mighty through God to the pulling down of strong holds;) casting down imaginations, and every high thing that exalteth itself against the knowledge of God, and bringing into captivity every thought to the obedience of Christ" (2 Corinthians 10:4–5 KJV).

"Behold God, my salvation! I will trust and not be afraid, for the Lord God is my strength and song; yes, He has become my salvation. Therefore with joy will you draw water from the wells of salvation" (Isaiah 12:2–3 AMPLIFIED).

"Rejoice in the Lord always—delight, gladden yourselves in Him; again I say, Rejoice!" (Philippians 4:4 AMPLIFIED).

"Although the fig tree shall not blossom, neither shall fruit be in the vines; the labour of the olive shall fail, and the fields shall yield no meat; the flock shall be cut off from the fold, and there shall be no herd in the stalls: Yet I will rejoice in the Lord, I will joy in the God of my salvation. The Lord God is my strength, and he will make my feet like hinds' feet, and he will make me to walk upon mine high places" (Habakkuk 3:17–19 KJV).

"Heal me, O Lord, and I shall be healed; save me, and I shall be saved; for you are my praise" (Jeremiah 17:14 NRSV).

"Thou wilt keep him in perfect peace, whose mind is stayed on thee: because he trusteth in thee" (Isaiah 26:3 KJV).

"Our inner selves wait [earnestly] for the Lord; He is our help and our shield. For in Him does our heart rejoice, because we have trusted (relied on and been

confident) in His holy name" (Psalm 33:20–21 AMPLI-
FIED).

"For He (God) Himself has said, I will not in any
way fail you nor give you up nor leave you without
support. [I will] not . . . in any degree leave you helpless, nor forsake nor let [you] down, [relax My hold on
you].—Assuredly not!" (Hebrews 13:5 AMPLIFIED).

"For I am persuaded beyond doubt—am sure—
that neither death, nor life, nor angels, nor principal-
ities, nor things impending and threatening, nor
things to come, nor powers, nor height, nor depth, nor
anything else in all creation will be able to separate
us from the love of God which is in Christ Jesus our
Lord" (Romans 8:38–39, AMPLIFIED).

Appendix II

Selected Writings of Catherine Marshall

During her career, Catherine wrote more than twenty books. Four of them were bestsellers: *A Man Called Peter, To Live Again, Beyond Our Selves*, and *Christy*. She also wrote dozens of articles for various Christian magazines. Her books have sold over two million copies in hardcover editions and continue to be popular fifteen years after her death. The following is a list and a brief synopsis of her most well-known books.

From Peter Marshall's sermons:
(1) *Mr. Jones, Meet the Master*
    This book is a compilation of twelve of Peter Marshall's most penetrating sermons. After much thought and preparation, Catherine decided to present Peter's sermons as close as possible to his original manuscripts, especially preserving the style in which he wrote them.
(2) *The Prayers of Peter Marshall*
    A compilation of Peter Marshall's prayers, in-

cluding many that he offered as chaplain of the Senate. Peter's spiritual boldness and sensitivity are clearly seen in this remarkable book.

(3) *Let's Keep Christmas* (Introduction by Catherine Marshall)

"One of the most beloved ministers of this century reminds us that Christmas means the birth of Jesus Christ—the gift of God with us. Marshall also celebrates the family customs that make the holiday so special. Wonderfully illustrated, this Christmas keepsake will be enjoyed by both children and adults."

(4) *The First Easter*

"Peter Marshall's sermons proved him to be not only a devout man of God but also a stimulating, sparkling storyteller. In this beloved book, Catherine Marshall skillfully weaves a magnificent dramatic narrative of Easter from Peter's many thought-provoking messages."

Books by Catherine Marshall (arranged by *original* date of publication):

(1) *A Man Called Peter*

"The story of Peter Marshall is an irresistible account of the love between a dynamic man and his God, and the tender romance between a man and a woman. It recounts the triumph of the young Scottish immigrant who made his way from his homeland to the chaplaincy of the United States Senate. Catherine and Peter's life together in the "halls of highest human happiness," as Peter often referred to marriage, is related with love, humor, and wisdom" (Chosen Books, 1951).

(2) *To Live Again*

This is an exciting story of how Catherine "won

her battle against grief and loneliness. It provides inspiring answers, not only for those who have known trouble and disappointment, but for everyone who seeks to live with wisdom and courage" (Chosen Books, 1957).

(3) *Beyond Our Selves*

This book covers a variety of events from Catherine's life, including her childhood and her marriage to Peter Marshall. She also discusses topics such as suffering, miracles, unanswered prayer, and healing. She wrote this book before her experience with Amy Catherine. It is interesting to compare insights in this book to the ones in *Something More*, which was written after the death of her granddaughter. (1961)

(4) *Christy*

This bestselling first person novel is a story about a young schoolteacher who goes to Cutter Gap in the Smoky Mountains to run a school. The story was inspired by Catherine's mother, Leonora Whitaker Wood. It is full of adventure, drama, and excitement. (1967)

(5) *Something More*

This book is a powerful account of Catherine's spiritual quests, personal tragedies, and her search for truth through faith in the Sovereign God. She discusses such topics as forgiveness, obedience, healing, dreams, and spiritual warfare. (1974)

(6) *Adventures in Prayer*

"In this classic, Catherine shares her personal discoveries about how surprisingly down-to-earth God wants our prayers to be. Her practical guidance on the basics of prayer includes specific prayers at the end of every chapter" (Chosen Books, 1975).

(7) *The Helper*

In this book Catherine "shares forty aspects of the Holy Spirit, combined with her own prayers and suggested Bible readings." Catherine's treatment of the Holy Spirit is both spiritually insightful and practically down-to-earth. (1978)

(8) *Meeting God at Every Turn*

"Catherine's central discovery through twelve encounters with her Lord traced in this book—from which she draws twelve life principles—is that it is possible for any of us to have a personal relationship with Him. Her suggested approach: Come to Him stripped of pretensions, with a needy, receptive spirit" (Chosen Books, 1980).

(9) *Julie*

A novel about Julie Wallace, an eighteen-year-old senior who is an up-and-coming reporter for her father's small paper. The conflicts in the story center on Julie herself. Another tense situation draws attention when a dam in the area collapses. Catherine's personality shines forth in Julie, which makes her character even more interesting and provocative. The eight-hundred page draft of this novel was completed only a few months before her death. (1984)

(10) *A Closer Walk*

Published a few years after Catherine's death, this book reveals her spiritual lifeline to God in selections from her personal journal. It is filled with the spiritual understanding that guided her in her attempts to overcome many personal challenges such as her nagging fear of death. (1986)

(11) *Light in My Darkest Night*
> This book is one of the most profound and re-
> vealing Marshall ever wrote. It is a compilation
> of her personal journal entries in which she
> worked through the pain and disappointment of
> the death of her granddaughter, Amy Catherine.
> Also eloquently portrayed is the way in which the
> Lord brought light and hope back into her life.
> (1989)

Bibliography

LeSourd, Leonard E., ed. *The Best of Catherine Marshall*. New York: Walker and Company, 1993.

Marshall, Catherine. *Something More*. New York: Guidepost Associates Inc., 1974.

———. *The Helper*. reprint ed. Grand Rapids, Mich.: Chosen Books, 1984.

———. *Adventures in Prayer*. reprint ed. Grand Rapids, Mich.: Chosen Books, 1985.

———. *Light in My Darkest Night*. Grand Rapids, Mich.: Chosen Books, 1989.

———. *The Inspirational Writings of Catherine Marshall: A Closer Walk*. Corvallis, Ore.: Arrowood Press, 1991.

———. *Beyond Our Selves*. reprint ed. Grand Rapids, Mich.: Fleming H. Revell, 1994.

———. *A Man Called Peter*. reprint ed. Grand Rapids, Mich.: Chosen Books, 1995.

———. *Meeting God at Every Turn: A Spiritual Autobiography*. reprint ed. Grand Rapids, Mich.: Chosen Books, 1995.

———. *To Live Again*. reprint ed. Grand Rapids, Mich.: Chosen Books, 1996.

Acknowledgments

I want to thank first and foremost Jesus Christ for allowing me the opportunity to write about a woman of such depth of Christian character. I also want to especially thank Steve Laube and Bethany House Publishers for believing in me enough to give me a second chance to write for them.

I also deeply appreciate and want to acknowledge the entire Marquez family—Dan, Mindy, Marissa, Justin, Devin, Megan, and Morgan—for watching over my children while I wrote this book and for making them feel like a part of the family.